Robert L Galloway

A History of Coal Mining in Great Britain

Robert L Galloway

A History of Coal Mining in Great Britain

ISBN/EAN: 9783743319684

Manufactured in Europe, USA, Canada, Australia, Japa

Cover: Foto ©ninafisch / pixelio.de

Manufactured and distributed by brebook publishing software (www.brebook.com)

Robert L Galloway

A History of Coal Mining in Great Britain

PREFACE.

In the following pages an endeavour is made to delineate the principal features in the growth of the great coal industry, with special reference to improvements in engineering, by means of which it has become possible for the miners to open out their deep "subterranean cities" and to procure and bring to the surface the vast quantities of coal which are now annually drawn from the mines of this country.

Apart from the value of coal as the mainspring of the great industrial pre-eminence of the kingdom, it is hoped that the narrative may not be without interest of another kind, inasmuch as it furnishes an account of the origin of some of the most useful inventions of modern times—as, for example railways, the steam-engine, and the locomotive—which were almost called into existence by mining requirements, and were long employed by the mining community before they came to be adopted, in a more improved form, by the public in general.

At no time were more vigorous efforts being made to promote the safety of the miners in their dangerous occupation than at present. Should the account here given of what has been accomplished in this direction tend to throw any light upon the matter, the circumstance would afford the writer the greatest satisfaction.

RYTON-ON-TYNE,
    9th May, 1882.

CONTENTS.

CHAPTER I.

PAGE

COAL LATE OF COMING INTO COMMON USE. FIRST EMPLOYED BY ARTISANS. ITS USE IN LONDON PROHIBITED BY ROYAL PROCLAMATION 1

CHAPTER II.

COAL COMES INTO USE FOR DOMESTIC PURPOSES IN THE COAL DISTRICTS. NUMBERS OF COLLIERIES OPENED OUT IN THE NEWCASTLE-ON-TYNE COAL-FIELD. KING EDWARD III. PATRONIZES AND REGULATES THE COAL TRADE. EARLY COAL MINING 11

CHAPTER III.

THE INCREASING SCARCITY OF WOOD CAUSES COAL TO COME INTO GENERAL USE FOR DOMESTIC PURPOSES. FIRST DIFFICULTIES IN THE MINES 19

CHAPTER IV.

COMBINATION AMONG THE COAL-OWNERS AT NEWCASTLE. TAXES IMPOSED ON COAL. THE HEARTH-MONEY OR CHIMNEY TAX. THE COAL FLEET 28

CHAPTER V.

DIFFICULTIES EXPERIENCED IN SUBSTITUTING COAL FOR WOOD AND CHARCOAL IN MANUFACTURING PROCESSES, MORE ESPECIALLY IN THE SMELTING OF IRON 36

CHAPTER VI.

INCREASE OF MINING DIFFICULTIES. IMPROVEMENTS IN MINING APPLIANCES. INVENTION OF RAILWAYS . . 52

CHAPTER VII.

NOXIOUS GASES PREVALENT IN THE MINES. ACCIDENTS OCCASIONED THEREBY. SMALL EXPLOSIONS OF FIRE-DAMP BECOME FREQUENT 68

CHAPTER VIII.

INADEQUACY OF THE WATER-RAISING MACHINERY. INVENTION OF THE STEAM-ENGINE 76

CONTENTS.

CHAPTER IX.

STATE OF MINING AT THE COMMENCEMENT OF THE EIGHTEENTH CENTURY. FIRST GREAT EXPLOSIONS IN THE NORTH OF ENGLAND COLLIERIES 83

CHAPTER X.

THE COAL TRADE OF THE WEST COAST. WHITEHAVEN MINES. CARLISLE AND JAMES SPEDDING. INVENTION OF THE STEEL MILL, AND COURSING THE AIR 91

CHAPTER XI.

REVIVAL OF THE IRON TRADE. GREAT BUILDING OF STEAM-ENGINES IN THE NORTH OF ENGLAND. INCREASING DEPTH OF THE PITS. VARIOUS APPLIANCES FOR VENTILATING THE MINES. EXPLOSIONS OF FREQUENT OCCURRENCE 101

CHAPTER XII.

FIRST EMPLOYMENT OF IRON IN RAILWAY CONSTRUCTION. THE STEAM-ENGINE INDIRECTLY APPLIED TO DRAW THE COAL OUT OF THE PITS THROUGH THE MEDIUM OF WATER-WHEELS. CURR'S IMPROVEMENTS IN SHAFT FITTINGS AND UNDERGROUND CONVEYANCE 109

CHAPTER XIII.

GREAT DIFFICULTIES ENCOUNTERED IN OPENING OUT THE FAMOUS WALLSEND COLLIERY. JOHN BUDDLE, SEN. CAST-IRON TUBBING 121

CHAPTER XIV.

VARIOUS METHODS OF DEALING WITH INFLAMMABLE GAS. THE DILUTING SYSTEM, THE NEUTRALIZING SYSTEM, THE FIRING SYSTEM, THE DRAINING SYSTEM . . . . 13.

CHAPTER XV.

THE SYSTEM OF COURSING THE AIR BECOMES INADEQUATE. CREEPS. MR. BUDDLE INTRODUCES COMPOUND OR DOUBLE VENTILATION, AND PANEL-WORKING 142

CHAPTER XVI.

INVENTION OF THE SAFETY-LAMP 153

CHAPTER XVII.

EXTENDED USE OF THE STEAM-ENGINE; THE LOCOMOTIVE; STEAM-BOATS. INTRODUCTION OF GAS LIGHTING 182

CHAPTER XVIII.

DEEPER AND MORE DIFFICULT WINNINGS 203

CHAPTER XIX.

INVENTION OF CAGES, AND IRON-WIRE ROPES . 211

CHAPTER XX.

INTERVENTION OF THE LEGISLATURE IN MINING OPERATIONS . 220

CHAPTER XXI.

GREAT IMPROVEMENT IN THE VENTILATION OF COLLIERIES. THE STEAM JET TRIED AND ABANDONED. MECHANICAL VENTILATORS COME INTO EXTENSIVE USE 247

CHAPTER XXII.

RECENT INVENTIONS, EXPERIMENTS, AND IMPROVEMENTS . . 257

CHAPTER XXIII.

MODERN MINING. MEASURES OF SAFETY AGAINST EXPLOSION . 265

A HISTORY OF COAL MINING
IN
GREAT BRITAIN.

CHAPTER I.

COAL LATE OF COMING INTO COMMON USE.—FIRST EMPLOYED BY ARTISANS.—ITS USE IN LONDON PROHIBITED BY ROYAL PROCLAMATION.

οὔτε νήσους οἶδα Κασσιτερίδας ἐούσας, ἐκ τῶν ὁ κασσίτερος ἡμῖν φοιτᾷ·—HERODOTUS.

IN the early dawn of history Britain was already celebrated for its mineral productions. Centuries before the commencement of the Christian era Phœnician traders sailed hither for supplies of tin—a metal then as now a peculiar product of the Land's End district. It was in connection with the traffic in this metal that our country made its first appearance on the page of history, and received from ancient writers the name of Cassiterides, or Tin Islands.

But though we possess records relative to the working of tin and other metals in Britain at a remote period, we know little regarding the ancient history of our coal; indeed, it is evident that the employment of coal fuel to any extent is of comparatively very modern date. It seems clear that the Romans were not wholly unacquainted with it during their occupation of the country, from the fact of small quantities of coal and coal ashes having been found among the ruins of many of their stations.[1] It is not, however, until a period long subsequent to their departure that this mineral begins to appear among other commodities as an article of merchandise, and to be referred to in terms which are clear and unmistakable.

The venerable Bede, who flourished at Jarrow on the southern bank of the river Tyne in the early part of the eighth century, gives us no hint of the use of coal fuel in the north at the time when he wrote. It is true that in speaking of the mineral products of the country he mentions the stone *gagates* (jet) as existing in great abundance; and under this term may perhaps be included the coal so plentifully found in the district where he lived. But to the use of this mineral for

---

[1] The "many beds of cinders" heaped up in the fields in the neighbourhood of North Brierly, in the West Riding of Yorkshire, mentioned by Whitaker, the historian of Manchester, is not a case in point, as they were not composed of the ashes of coal, as he erroneously supposes, but of the *scoriæ*, or slag, of Roman ironworks.

fuel he makes no allusion, though he notes that when kindled it had the property of driving off serpents.[1]

The abundant records of the twelfth century which have come down to us seem to show that even at this period wood, charcoal, and peat, continued to be the fuel universally employed for all purposes; and this century was far advanced, if not quite ended, before we meet with any reliable indications of a commencement having been made to bring mineral coal into use.

In the early Norman era the internal arrangements of common dwelling-houses precluded the use of coal for domestic purposes. Chimneys are mentioned as a new feature which had been introduced into the Norman castles and houses, the massive walls of which admitted of flues being carried up in their thickness. But they were unknown in the houses of the common people. The walls of these were of wood. The fire-place consisted of a cavity in the centre of the floor, which was covered over when the fire was out; and at this time it was enacted by law that all fires should be extinguished at a certain hour in the evening, notified by the ringing of a bell, termed from this circumstance the *curfew* (couvre feu). The smoke from fires so situated pervaded the whole apartment, and made its escape by

---

[1] The oft-quoted passage in the *Anglo-Saxon Chronicle* in which coal is supposed to be referred to under the name *græfan* is at best equivocal, inasmuch as peat is graven, or dug, as well as coal. It seems more probable that the former is alluded to.

a hole in the roof, or by the doorway—a primitive arrangement to be met with even at the present day in some parts of the Highlands of Scotland and west of Ireland, where peat fuel is still employed. Under such conditions it is obvious that the use of coal in the interior of dwellings was altogether inadmissible.

The obscurity which prevails regarding the employment of coal fuel in early times begins to vanish about the end of the twelfth century, and from this epoch we may date the commencement of the great modern coal trade.

Both in England and Scotland coal appears first to have received attention at points where the carboniferous strata were exposed on the sea shore: a circumstance which seems the most probable origin of the name *sea coal*, by which the mineral was so long and so widely known, in contradistinction to charcoal, to which the name *coal* was originally applied.

Conditions peculiarly favourable to the early working of coal existed on the sea coast of Northumberland, and on the shores of the Frith of Forth. In both cases it could be alike easily got (as the coal seams came out to the surface) and easily conveyed to market: a state of things well calculated to promote the growth of a trade in the mineral on its first coming into use. Historical records point to these localities as the cradles of the coal trade.

Before the close of the reign of William the Lion

(which terminated 1214 A.D.), we find coal beginning to receive attention on the south shore of the Frith of Forth. Thus among the grants made to the monks of Holyrood Abbey, Edinburgh, during this reign, one consists of the tithe of the colliery of Carriden, near Blackness, given along with the tithe of the proceeds of the harbour at the same place. This grant was confirmed by King William, and is supposed to have been made before the end of the twelfth century. In the same reign (between 1210–14 A.D.) the monks of Newbottle Abbey received the grant of a colliery and quarry on the sea shore at Preston, in the lands of Tranent, a district which from this early period downwards continued to be famed for its production of coal.

There appear to be no certain allusions to the existence of a coal trade in England previous to the termination of the conflict between King John and the barons, when by the granting of the Magna Charta (1215 A.D.) a greatly increased security was given to subjects in the possession of their lands and rights. Soon after this period, and without any special concession on the part of the Crown, we have evidence of a commencement having been made to work coal, and to carry it from the north to London. As early as the year 1228 a lane in a suburb of the metropolis is mentioned under the name of "Sacoles Lane" (*i.e.* Sea Coals Lane), clearly showing that some trade in coal was now going on there. This lane was also called Lime-burner's Lane, and it is well known that the burning of lime was one of the earliest uses to which mineral coal was applied.

At almost exactly the same date, at all events as early as the year 1236, we find the monks of Newminster Abbey, near Morpeth in Northumberland, receiving a grant of some land on the sea shore near Blyth, with a right of way to the shore to obtain sea weed for tillage and sea coal wherever it might be found.

The purpose for which the coal was intended is not specified in the above grant, but a few years later (about 1240 A.D.) the same monks received another charter in which sea coal formed the special subject; and in this case the coal is stated to be conceded for the use of *the forge* at one of their granges.

From this time forward references to the working and use of coal become sufficiently numerous. To the town of Newcastle-on-Tyne in particular the new trade soon became productive of considerable benefit. Newcastle had been a place of some importance during the Roman occupation of the country, under the name of Pons Ælii—Ælius being the family name of the Emperor Hadrian, who built the great wall from the Tyne to the Solway Frith, about 120 A.D. In the Dark Ages it became the seat of a colony of monks, and took the name of Monkchester. The modern town grew up under the protection of the Norman Castle built to guard the approach to the bridge across the Tyne. This was termed the *new* castle, in contradistinction to the ancient fortifications on the site of which it was placed, and the town of which it formed the nucleus received its name from it.

Newcastle was at first under the jurisdiction of the sheriff of Northumberland, who paid an annual rent of 50*l.* for it to the Crown, recouping himself out of the tolls and customs arising from its trade; but in the year 1213 the burgesses succeeded in obtaining the management of the town into their own hands, holding it direct from the Crown at an annual rent of 100*l.*, though at the time it was hardly worth so much. As yet there appears to have been no coal trade on the Tyne.

Being a community of traders the burgesses of Newcastle looked with no favourable eye on the trading proclivities of their neighbours, the Bishop of Durham and the Prior of Tynemouth, and were incessantly engaged in disputes with one or the other regarding the navigation of the Tyne. Not infrequently in the solution of disputed points the burgesses took the law into their own hands. The establishment of villages on the lands of the above prelates at North and South Shields, near the mouth of the Tyne, where it was alleged "no towns ought to be," was specially objectionable to the burgesses and the cause of frequent complaint. In connection with a skirmish which occurred at the former village we meet with one of the earliest allusions to the Tyne coal trade. At Newcastle in 1268-9 a number of persons were brought before the justices to answer to the Prior of Tynemouth, "wherefore they had come *vi et armis* to the Prior's mills at Shields, had burned down the mills, threatened and maltreated some of the Prior's monks whom they found there, and had seized and taken away a ship of the Prior's lying there laden with sea coal," besides committing further damages, for all which satisfaction was demanded by the Prior.

The increase in the revenue of the town of Newcastle, which took place during the course of the thirteenth century, owing to the rise of the coal trade, is evidenced by the return to an inquiry made in the year 1281, by order of King Edward I., from which we learn that the town was then at times worth 200*l*. per annum to the burgesses, the advance in its value being ascribed to the new trade in coal.

When the working of coal had once been commenced the opening out of collieries soon became general throughout the kingdom, and before the close of the reign of Edward I. (1307 A.D.) the mineral was being dug, though doubtless only on a small scale, in most of the coalfields of England, Wales, and Scotland.

In the early period of its history coal was employed

for few purposes. The only patrons of the new fuel at first were humble artisans, such as smiths and lime-burners, to whose requirements it was peculiarly well suited. From these it gradually spread to other classes of artificers who used furnaces in their trades.

By the bulk of the community coal fuel was regarded with much aversion on account of the disagreeable smoke to which it gave rise. Coal smoke was considered to be very detrimental to health. It began to be considered a source of annoyance while the coal trade was still in its infancy. Thus we learn from the annals of Dunstable that in the year 1257 Eleanor, Queen of Henry III., was obliged to leave the town of Nottingham, where she had been sent to stay during the absence of the King on an expedition into Wales, and removed to Tutbury Castle instead, being quite unable to remain in Nottingham on account of the smoke of the sea coals.

Half a century later great efforts were made to check the spread of the use of coal in London on the plea that it was an innovation on established custom and an intolerable nuisance on account of the smoke to which it gave rise. It appears that towards the end of the reign of Edward I. a great increase took place in the quantity of coal consumed in the metropolis; brewers, dyers, and others who required much fuel, having commenced to use it largely instead of wood and charcoal. But the consequence of the change told injuriously on the atmosphere of the city. The nobles, prelates, and others repairing to London to attend Parliament and for other purposes, were specially annoyed by the increasing smoke, and took the lead in getting up demonstrations against the obnoxious fuel, but the great body of the populace joined in the movement. In consequence of the agitation a Royal proclamation was issued in the year 1306 prohibiting artificers from using sea coal in their furnaces, and commanding them to return to the fuel which they had been accustomed to use. The proclamation, however, appears to have been little attended to by the brewers, dyers, &c., who had already formed a strong attachment to the new fuel. Complaints continuing to be made, it was determined to have recourse to stronger measures to put an end to the use of coal. In 1307 a commission of Oyer and Terminer was appointed, with instructions "to inquire of all such who burnt sea coal in the city, or parts adjoining, and to punish them for the first offence with great fines and ransoms, and upon the second offence to demolish their furnaces," and to see the proclamation strictly observed for the time to come.

CHAPTER II.

COAL COMES INTO USE FOR DOMESTIC PURPOSES IN THE COAL DISTRICTS.—NUMBERS OF COLLIERIES OPENED OUT IN THE NEWCASTLE-ON-TYNE COALFIELD.—KING EDWARD III. PATRONIZES AND REGULATES THE COAL TRADE.—EARLY COAL MINING.

"By the leading of coals of this kind to all places within our kingdom the greatest benefit will result to us and our people."— *Letters patent of King Edward III.*

In the beginning of the fourteenth century the coal trade continued to thrive and grow, particularly on the Tyne and the Frith of Forth, and to a smaller extent on the estuaries of the Dee and the Severn; while small workings at many points in the interior supplied the coal required in their own immediate neighbourhood.

Purchases of coal figure very commonly in the accounts of numerous castles in the course of erection at this period (*e.g.* Dunstanborough, Caernarvon, Beaumaris, &c.), being used by the smiths and lime-burners in connection with the building operations.

Even in the vicinity of the metropolis we find these classes continuing to employ coal without hindrance. Thus in the year 1316 a sum of money was paid out of the Royal Exchequer to one John de Norton, surveyor of works at Westminster Palace, to purchase iron, steel, and sea coal to make divers heads for the king's lances. A little later (1329 A.D.), proceedings were taken before the Lord Mayor of London against Hugh de Hecham, "lymbrenmere," for entering into a conspiracy with his fellows to force up the price of lime in the London market; the evidence of his extortionate charges being that whereas formerly a sack of lime was sold for a penny, when sea coal was at 40d. the quarter, now he refused to sell any sack for less than 1½d. or 2d., though the price of sea coal had fallen to 16d.

As early as the reign of Edward II., a commencement was made to export coal from the Tyne to France. Mention occurs of a vessel belonging to the town of Pontoise as bringing a cargo of corn to Newcastle-on-Tyne in 1325, and returning freighted with sea coal.

But the most interesting matter connected with the coal trade during the first half of the fourteenth century is the fact that mineral fuel then began to be partially employed for domestic purposes in the coal districts. As the monks were among the first to open out collieries, so they appear to have taken the lead in admitting the new fuel into their dwellings. We find the monks of Jarrow Monastery using coal in the year

1313, and soon after this date a mixture of wood and coal became the fuel commonly employed in localities where a cheap and plentiful supply of the latter could be obtained.

The difficulties in the way of using coal for domestic purposes appear to have been overcome by improvements in the arrangements of the fire-hearth, and perhaps more immediately by the employment of iron fire-grates or "chimneys" as they were termed. The building of fire-places of stone in the case of wooden houses, or in that of houses not provided with flues in the walls, could obviously not have been accomplished without considerable difficulty and expense. The "iron chimney," on the other hand, could be employed in any house, or even in any part of the house. It was not a fixture attached to the wall like the modern grate, but loose and movable from room to room. These iron chimneys soon came much into use. We are told that they were considered a very important piece of furniture, and were frequently entailed by will upon son after son in succession. Associated with them we find mention of the familiar poker and tongs; these implements of the smith's craft having accompanied mineral fuel in its passage from the forge into a wider sphere in ordinary house fires.

The coal trade was now becoming established on a broader basis, and the steady increase in the demand for coal which ensued gave rise to the opening out of numerous additional collieries. In the Great Northern coalfield (of Northumberland and Durham), many mines were brought into operation during the course of the fourteenth century, particularly on the banks of the Tyne, where peculiar natural facilities existed for carrying on a coal trade.

On the north side of the Tyne in the lands of Elswick, which lay immediately to the west of the town-lands of Newcastle-on-Tyne, we find the monks of Tynemouth, the owners of the royalty, letting various collieries on lease in 1330 and subsequent years. Shortly afterwards (1351), the burgesses of Newcastle obtained a licence from King Edward III. to work the coal in two portions of the town-lands, named the Castle-field and the Frith,[1] in order to aid them in the payment of their annual rent, the town having suffered severely in common with other parts of the kingdom from the pestilence which ravaged England in the middle of this century. A few years later (1358), the king likewise granted the burgesses the coal in the Town Moor for the same object.

In addition to the collieries on the north side of the Tyne, a considerable number of mines on its southern bank poured supplies of coal into the market at Newcastle. In 1356, the Bishop of Durham had five mines

---

[1] This grant is usually stated to have been made by Henry III. more than a century earlier. The error originated with Gardner in 1656, and has ever since passed current.

let on lease in the Manor of Whickham, and others at Gateshead; and in the surrounding district the working of coal was actively going on at Birtley, Fugerhous, and Winlaton.

Edward III. was the first king to interest himself in the Tyne coal trade, his attention being frequently drawn to the subject in various ways, more especially in connection with disputes regarding the shipment of coal. He issued several writs for the regulation of the trade, and granted letters of protection to the owners of collieries on the south side of the Tyne by which they were allowed to carry their coal across the river to Newcastle, and after paying the customs of the port, to take them to any part of the kingdom or to Calais, which was at this period the only place on the Continent to which the staple commodities of England were allowed to be exported. He also gave his sanction to coal being loaded by the *keel* instead of being measured in the detailed manner which appears to have been employed while the trade was insignificant.

The keel is a class of vessel peculiar to the Tyne, and to the coal trade. It is a broad flat-bottomed boat of oval form, designed to carry the heaviest load with the least draught of water. Its name and origin are both Saxon, and its history goes back to the advent of the Saxons in England, Verstegan informing us that the first detachment of Saxons crossed from the Continent in three keels. The size of the keel used in the coal trade was fixed near the end of the fourteenth century. At this period it carried twenty chaldrons of coal, on each of which a duty of 2*d*. was paid to the Crown by merchants and strangers not possessed of the freedom of Newcastle. But while the size of the keel has remained the same down to the present day (about twenty-one tons), the size of the Newcastle chaldron (on which the duty was paid), was gradually much increased until fixed by law long afterwards when it had attained to upwards of twice its original proportions.

Not only on the banks of the Tyne but at many different points in the Great Northern coalfield the working of coal was being carried on in the latter half of the fourteenth century. Already at this time collieries had been opened out at Lumley, Cocken, and Rainton, on the River Wear; and further south at Hett, Coxhoe, Coundon, Evenwood, Softley, and Cockfield Fell. We also hear of coal mines at Plessey, near Blyth, in Northumberland: and have evidence of small collieries being worked in other parts of the same county.

In the system of mining no less than in the coal trade matters were already assuming a settled form at this epoch. The holes and quarries from which the supplies of coal were at first obtained had in the middle of the fourteenth century been superseded by regular mine works, consisting of *pit and adit*, or vertical shaft and horizontal gallery. This arrangement was simple and effective, and remained the typical form so long as coal workings were only carried on above the level of free drainage. The shaft was employed for raising the coal by means of a windlass, or jack roll, worked by manual labour; the adit,[1] or water-gate, served to drain off the water from the workings; while the two combined produced a natural ventilation sufficient for the shallow and limited workings of these early times.

Even at this period coal leases were beginning to be drawn out with considerable care and detail. In the earliest leases of which we find mention (such as those granted by the monks of Tynemouth about 1330 A.D.), a certain rent per annum was alone reserved by the lessors, without any stipulation as to the quantity of coal allowed to be worked for the same. But the necessity of making the quantity of coal drawn from the mine bear a fixed relation to the amount of rent paid soon became felt, and as early as the middle of the fourteenth century provisions were introduced for this purpose. At first this was effected by simply limiting the quantity of coal which might be worked. Thus in a lease of five mines at Whickham, made by the Bishop of Durham in 1356, it was stipulated that the lessees might not draw from each mine more than *one keel*

---

[1] This word occurs in a variety of forms which seem to point to its being a contraction for *aqueduct*.

(twenty-one tons) per day. The arrangement of limiting the quantity of coal to be worked was the plan usually adopted in leases, until the introduction of the more improved modern method of having both a fixed and a sliding, or tonnage rent, which makes the amount of rent to be in exact proportion to the quantity of coal worked.

CHAPTER III.

THE INCREASING SCARCITY OF WOOD CAUSES COAL TO COME INTO GENERAL USE FOR DOMESTIC PURPOSES.—FIRST DIFFICULTIES IN THE MINES.

> "Thou didst swear to me . . . sitting by a sea-coal fire."
> —SHAKSPEARE.

A SCARCITY of materials appears to exist relative to the coal trade during the fifteenth century, but not so with reference to the mines, and we have evidence of a steady increase in the demand for coal from the gradual extension of mining operations which was going on, many new coal tracts being brought under contribution. The extension, however, was on the same lines as before; the supplies of coal were still obtained from shallow workings; while the produce of the mines was chiefly consumed by the inhabitants of the coal districts, or of the maritime towns, or exported to the Continent.

By those altogether unaccustomed to it, the use of stones for fuel was regarded with curiosity. Æneas

Sylvius (afterwards Pope Pius II.), who visited Scotland in the capacity of papal legate in the middle of the fifteenth century, mentions in his *Commentaries* that he saw the poor people who begged at the churches going away quite pleased with stones given them for alms. "This kind of stone," he adds, "being impregnated with sulphur or some fatty matter, is burnt instead of wood, of which the country is destitute."

Even about a century later it seemed to surprise Leland to find the population of the English coal districts using coals in their fires in places where supplies of wood could still be had. He explains the circumstance by stating that coal was found plentifully there, and "sold good chepe."

During the sixteenth century the coal trade entered upon a period of greatly increased activity. A considerable demand for coal had sprung up on the Continent, and large quantities were exported thither from the Tyne and the Frith of Forth. In the year 1546 we find an order sent to Newcastle by King Henry VIII. for 3,000 chaldrons of coal to be forwarded to Boulogne, in France, with all possible despatch. Artificers in France were already relying to a large extent on supplies of coal from Newcastle. A letter written in 1552 speaks of Newcastle coal as "that thinge that France can lyve no more withowte than the fyshe without water," for without this, says the writer, "they can nother make stele worke, nor metall worke, nor wyer worke, nor goldsmythe worke, nor gunnes, nor no manner of thinge that passeth the fier."

The exportation of coal appears to have been a very lucrative trade at this period. We hear of it being bought at Newcastle for 2s. 2d. per chaldron and sold in France at thirteen nobles, or 4l. 6s. 8d. But the scarcity of fuel at home caused this drain upon the resources of the country to be viewed with a degree of alarm. The question of prohibiting the export of coal was under the consideration of the English Parliament in 1549, and was frequently discussed from time to time during subsequent years. One proposal made was that all the best coal should be kept at home, but that foreigners might have the benefit of the inferior sorts. No actual steps, however, appear to have been taken to check the export trade in England, but in Scotland, where the decay of the "coal heuchs" was already becoming a source of anxiety, and the gravest fears were entertained of the speedy exhaustion of the coal fields, an Act of Parliament was passed in 1563 prohibiting all persons from transporting coals out of the realm under penalty of confiscation of the ship and cargo. This Act sets forth that coals were becoming the common ballast of all empty ships, which was occasioning "a maist exorbitant dearth and scantnesse of fewall." Licences to export coal were subsequently purchased by certain families, who realised large fortunes from the monopoly.

A factor still more important than the exportation of coal in the increased activity of the coal trade at this period was the rapid spread of the use of coal for domestic purposes which was now taking place. Notwithstanding the abundance of wood which had existed in England—so much so that it was considered impossible there should ever be any scarcity of it—the supplies were beginning to fail. To add to the difficulties of the wood-consuming portion of the population, the iron trade at the same time received a great impulse from the introduction of the process of making *cast iron*, which was followed by a great demand for large cast iron cannon —the earlier cannon having been manufactured from bars of wrought iron hooped together :[1] an imperfect arrangement which caused them to become disabled after firing a few rounds. The principal seats of the iron trade at this period were in the thickly-wooded districts of the weald, or wild, in the south-eastern counties of Kent, Surrey, and Sussex, and all the iron made in the country was smelted with charcoal. Repeated Acts of Parliament were passed for the preservation of woods, and restraining the "voragious" iron furnaces, but they proved of little avail. Wood fuel rapidly became scarcer and dearer, and coal as rapidly supplanted it in the market.

Thus it happened that during the reign of Queen Elizabeth, and in the space of little more than a

---

[1] A huge antique piece of orduance of this kind, named "Mons Meg," is still preserved at Edinburgh Castle.

generation, the relative positions of wood fuel, and coal underwent quite a reversal. The change was not brought about by choice, but by necessity. Elderly people who clung to the usages to which they had been accustomed in their youth regarded the great building of chimneys which was going on as an indication of the degeneracy of the times and the cause of numerous ills. They were so much attached to the smoky atmosphere of their dwellings that they were loth to part with it for the clearer air which resulted from the use of chimneys. Lamenting the decadence of the age in this and other respects, Harrison, writing in 1577, observes:—

"Now we have many chimnyes, and yet our tenderlings complaine of rewmes, catarres, and poses; then had we none but reredoses, and our heads did never ake. For as the smoke in those days was supposed to be a sufficient hardening for the timber of the house, so it was reputed a far better medicine to keep the good man and his family from the quacke and the pose, wherewith as then very few were acquainted. There are old men yet dwelling in the village where I remain, which have noted the multitude of chimnies lately erected, whereas in their young days there was not above two or three, if so many, in most uplandish towns of the realme (the religious houses and mannour places of their lordes always excepted, and peradventure some great personages), but each one made his fire against a reredosse in the halle where he dined and dressed his meate. When our houses were buylded of willowe then we had oken men, but nowe that our houses are come to be made of oke, our men are not only become willow, but a great many altogether of straw, which is a sore alteration."

Under the pressure of necessity people were all beginning to use coal instead of wood towards the close of the sixteenth century. The once banished fuel now found its way back into the furnaces of the London brewers, as we learn from a petition presented to the Council, in 1578, by the Company of Brewers, wherein they offer to use wood only in the brewhouses nearest Westminster Palace, as they understand that the Queen findeth "hersealfe greately greved and anoyed with the taste and smoke of the sea cooles." It also about the same time began to obtain admission into some of "the greatest merchants' parlours." And in a note of the revenues of the Bishop of London, dated 1598, it is set forth that whereas his lordship's predecessors had derived no small part of their income from sales of wood, the present Bishop has to buy timber for repairs and "he has to burn sea coals."

The London ladies were very reluctant to acquiesce in the change of fuel, and held out against it as long as possible. Writing in 1631, Howes tells us that "within thirty years last the nice dames of London would not come into any house or room when sea coals were burned, nor willingly eat of the meat that was either sod or roasted with sea coal fire." Even they, however, now withdrew their opposition, and coal at length became the fuel of the metropolis.

Within a few years after the commencement of the seventeenth century the change from wood fuel to coal, for domestic purposes, was general and complete; the latter, Howes tells us, being used in 1612 in the houses of the nobility, clergy, and gentry in London, and in all the other cities and shires of the kingdom, as well for the dressing of meat, washing, brewing, dyeing, as for other requirements.

Up to this time the supplies of coal had been obtained without its being necessary for the miners to penetrate far below the surface. In nearly every case the drainage of the mines was effected by means of the horizontal tunnels already mentioned, which were variously termed adits, watergates, soughs, surfs, &c., and these were considered very important adjuncts of the coal mines.

In some of the districts, however, where the mining of coal had been going on with most activity, symptoms due to increasing depth had already begun to make their appearance. Even before the end of the fifteenth century, at collieries on the Tyne and the Wear almost simultaneously, we hear of endeavours being made to push the pits below the water-level, and to raise the water by machinery. In the year 1486-7 the monks of Finchale Priory expended a sum of money at one of their collieries on the Wear "on the new ordinance of the pump" and in the purchase of horses for the same. And almost exactly at the same time a commencement was made to draw the water to the surface at a mine at Whickham on the Tyne, belonging to the Bishop of Durham. In the roll of the stock-keeper of the Bishopric for the year 1492-3, a payment is recorded for "two great iron chains for the ordinance of the mine at Whickham, for drawing coals and water out of the coal pit there, by my lord's command."

Other difficulties besides those arising from water were also beginning to embarrass the miners. Among these may be mentioned underground fires, several of which occurred in the sixteenth century. Thus at Coleorton, in Leicestershire, the coal was on fire and burnt many years during the reign of Henry VIII. The coal at Dysart, in Fifeshire, was on fire equally early and continued to burn for more than two centuries. Buchanan from this circumstance fixed on the neighbourhood of Dysart for the scene of the exorcism in his *Franciscanus et Fratres* (written in the reign of James V.), and describes the place as it appeared under one of those violent eruptions which are stated to have occurred periodically.

As the collieries became deeper and more extensive, the natural ventilation became more feeble and inconstant, and noxious gases began to imperil the safety of the miners. These gases we first hear of about the middle of the sixteenth century, writing at which time Dr. Kaye, or Keys (the founder of Caius College, Cambridge), speaks of certain coal pits in the northern parts of Britain, "the unwholesome vapour whereof is so pernicious to the hired labourers that it would immediately destroy them if they did not get out of the way as soon as the flame of their lamps becomes blue and is consumed."

In other respects the working of the collieries was conducted with great simplicity. The miner's tools consisted of the pick, the hammer and wedge, and the wooden shovel. The only machine in common use was the windlass for raising the buckets or baskets of coal in the shaft; and in the collieries in the east of Scotland even the windlass was unknown, the coals being carried up stairs in the shafts on the backs of women termed "coal-bearers." Above ground the produce was conveyed away from the mine either in ordinary wains, or in panniers on horseback, both methods being in common use.

CHAPTER IV.

COMBINATION AMONG THE COAL OWNERS AT NEW-CASTLE.—TAXES IMPOSED ON COAL.—THE HEARTH-MONEY OR CHIMNEY-TAX.—THE COAL FLEET.

"This great trade hath made this part to flourish in all trades."
—*Chorographia; or, A Survey of Newcastle-on-Tyne.*

ONE of the first consequences of the increased demand for coal, arising from its extended use for domestic purposes, was an advance in the price of the commodity. This was doubtless due at least in part to natural causes, but at the time it was wholly ascribed to a "combynation" among the colliery owners in the north, which was brought about in the following manner :—

In the year 1582 Queen Elizabeth obtained from the Bishop of Durham a lease of the manors of Gateshead and Whickham, with all the coal-pits, &c., for a term of ninety-nine years. This lease (called the Grand Lease) was procured from the Queen by the Earl of

Leicester, who transferred it to his secretary, Sir Thomas Sutton, the founder of the Charter House. Sutton again, for the sum of 12,000*l*., assigned his interest in the lease to the "Society of Free Hosts" of Newcastle-on-Tyne for the benefit of the town. The members of this society, about sixty in number, many of whom were coal owners, next compounded among themselves and made over their whole right to about eighteen or twenty, who having coal-pits of their own before engrossed the whole trade, and combined to sell coal at their own prices. These few persons, besides the Grand Lease, had secured all the principal mines about Newcastle, viz., Stella, the Bishop's Colliery, Ravensworth Colliery, Mr. Gascoigne's Colliery, Newburn Colliery, and others, of which they opened and shut up such and so many as they thought good.

While Sutton held the Grand Lease the price of coal of the best sort—which for a long time previously stood at 4*s*. per chaldron—rose to 6*s*.; and after this lease came into the possession of the town of Newcastle (1591 A.D.), the price rose successively to 7*s*., 8*s*., and 9*s*. On this the Lord Mayor of London protested to Lord Burleigh against the action of the northern coal owners, and requested an order from the Privy Council that all owners and farmers of coal-mines might open them and sell the coal at reasonable rates, not exceeding 7*s*. per chaldron, and might ship their coal at the most convenient places without any restraint. No steps, however, appear to have been taken beyond the summoning of two aldermen from Newcastle to explain the causes of the advance in the price of coal. The regulation of the trade, or "management of the v̲e̲n̲d̲" as it was termed, was in full force in the early part of the following century; and long continued to be a peculiar feature of the Tyne coal trade.

Some other attempts to establish coal monopolies were made at this period at Coventry in the Warwickshire coal-field, and at Bristol in Somersetshire, but these were merely of local importance.

Scarcely had the coal trade begun to assume more extended proportions before it became subjected to a system of heavy taxation. Reference has been made to a small ancient duty of 2d. per chaldron due to the Crown upon all coal sold to persons not franchised in the port of Newcastle. This, it seems, had for a length of time been neglected to be paid, and Queen Elizabeth demanded such arrears from the burgesses of Newcastle that they professed themselves unable to satisfy the claim, but offered instead to pay a duty of 1s. per chaldron for the future on all coal sold to the free people of England. The compromise was accepted by the Queen, and the duty continued to be levied during a long period. Under the name of "the Richmond shilling" (so termed on account of the proceeds arising from it being subsequently granted by Charles II. to his natural son the Duke of Richmond), it survived down till near the middle of the present century, when it was finally repealed.

Queen Elizabeth at the same time imposed a duty of 5s. per chaldron on all coal exported over sea. And for the better loading and disposing of coals and grindstones the Queen in the year 1600-1, by a clause in the great charter to Newcastle, incorporated the society of Hostmen, who had existed as a guild or fraternity in the town "from time immemorial." The origin of the Hostmen, or Free Hosts, appears to date from the year 1404, at which time it was ordained by statute that in every city, town, or seaport to which foreign merchants repaired, "hosts" should be appointed, with whom only the merchants might dwell during their stay.

From the books of the above society it appears that in 1602 there were twenty-eight acting "fitters," or hostmen, who were to vend by the year 9,080 tens of coal (or 190,680 tons), and to find eighty-five keels for the purpose; the prices fixed were for the best sort not above 10s., for the second best not above 9s., and for "meane coles" not above 8s. per chaldron.

During the two succeeding reigns additional taxes were imposed upon coal. King James added a duty of 3s. 4d. per chaldron on coals exported in foreign ships, and 1s. 8d. on coals exported in English ships. And Charles I. augmented the export duty by a further imposition of 4s. per chaldron. So prolific a source of revenue to the Crown had the coal taxes become, that in 1635 we find "the farm of sea coals" spoken of as "the bravest farm the King has."

But Charles I. was anxious to make the coal trade still further productive, and for this purpose he resolved to make himself the sole vendor of coals. This was seemingly an attempt to introduce into the coal trade a right of pre-emption similar to that already enjoyed by the Crown in the case of the tin trade. In 1638 an agreement was concluded between the King on the one part, and the colliery owners and hostmen on the other part, for all coals to be sold only to His Majesty, at the price of 11s. per chaldron for coals loaded into English, and 12s. for coals loaded into foreign vessels. An order of the Privy Council at the same time fixed the price of coals sold in London at 17s. per chaldron during the summer, and 19s. during the winter. Scarcely, however, had the monopoly been arranged for before the civil wars came on, and the whole organisation was broken up.

The great crop of chimneys which had sprung up throughout the kingdom did not escape the notice of the lynx-eyed tax-gatherers, and they, in common with the coal consumed in them, were brought under taxation. The hearth-money, or chimney-tax, was one of the most unpopular of taxes. It pressed heavily on the poor and lightly on the rich. Macaulay tells us that "the collectors were empowered to examine the interior of every house in the realm, to disturb families at meals, to force the doors of bedrooms, and, if the sum demanded were not punctually paid, to sell the trencher on which the barley loaf was divided among the poor children, and the pillow from under the head of the lying-in woman. Nor could the Treasury effectually restrain the chimneyman from using his powers with harshness; for the tax was farmed, and the government was consequently forced to connive at outrages and exactions such as have, in every age, made the name of publican a proverb for all that is most hateful."

The chimneyman was held in the greatest detestation by the housewives; on his approach they took the precaution to stow the cooking utensils out of sight.

"The good old dames whenever they the chimneyman espied
Unto their works they haste away, the pots and pipkins hide;
There is not one old dame in ten, search all the nation through,
But if you talk of chimneymen will spare a curse or two."

The chimney-tax was repealed in the reign of William III., and a tax on windows substituted for it.

The rapid spread of the use of coal during the reign of Queen Elizabeth called into existence a considerable fleet of vessels to carry on the traffic between the northern collieries and the metropolis, and other towns on the eastern seaboard. These vessels, which obtained the name of the "coal fleet," began to receive attention from the Government about the end of the sixteenth century, when, from their numbers and the importance of the trade in which they were engaged, the necessity of protecting them against enemies became obvious. In connection with the first proposal to provide an armed convoy for the coal fleet, made in the year 1596, we learn that the number of vessels engaged in the trade was then two hundred.

In 1615 the coal fleet numbered four hundred vessels, one half of which were required for the supply of London, and the remainder for other parts of the kingdom. A large export trade was also being carried on from the Tyne at this time by foreign vessels. "Besides our own ships," says a writer of the period, "hither, even to the mine's mouth, come all our neighbouring nations with their ships continually. The French sail thither in whole fleets of fifty sail together, serving all the parts of Picardie, Normandie, Bretagne, &c., even as far as Rochelle and Bourdeaux; and the ships of Bremen, Embden, Holland and Zealand, supply Flanders, &c., with our coals."

Twenty years later the coal fleet had increased to six or seven hundred ships, and was already regarded as "a great nursery of seamen." Still it continued to grow apace, and by the middle of the seventeenth century it had reached about nine hundred sail.

At this time it was confidently believed by many that supplies of coal could be got by sinking pits in Windsor Forest or Blackheath just as well as at Newcastle, and that the sole motive for bringing it from the north in preference was to maintain the coal fleet for rearing seamen for the navy. A lease of the coal in Windsor Forest was actually granted, but whether mining operations were really commenced there we are unable to say.

As London was now relying almost entirely for fuel on coal brought by sea, several times during the seventeenth century the city was reduced to great straits owing to temporary interruptions of the traffic. This was particularly the case in the years 1642–4, during the civil wars, and again in 1667 during the war with Holland, when the Dutch men-of-war "domineered" over the shores and prevented the colliers from putting out to sea. At the latter period coal rose in the metropolis to the famine price of 6*l*. per chaldron, and the complaints occasioned by the scarcity of fuel are described as "great and unspeakable." Near the end of this century the quantity of coal annually consumed in London had reached 400,000 chaldrons, or about half a million of tons.

CHAPTER V.

DIFFICULTIES EXPERIENCED IN SUBSTITUTING COAL FOR WOOD AND CHARCOAL IN MANUFACTURING PROCESSES, MORE ESPECIALLY IN THE SMELTING OF IRON.

> "Alas, what perils do environ
> All men that meddle with hot iron!"
> —*Anon.*

THE same causes which led to the adoption of coal as a substitute for wood in house fires, led in like manner to its gradual adoption for all other purposes of fuel. But in some branches of trade much greater difficulty was experienced in making the change than in others, involving as it did the invention of new arrangements and different processes, or even the removal of the industry altogether to new localities.

Among the manufactures, glass-making was one of the earliest to abandon wood for coal. But little glass was made in England as late as the middle of the reign of Queen Elizabeth, and the little that was made was manufactured in Sussex with wood fuel. A writer of the period (1577) tells us that—

> "As for glass-makers they be scant in this land,
> Yet one there is as I do understand,
> And in Sussex is now his habitation,
> At Chiddingsfold he works of his occupation."

Other glass-houses were established soon after this date, but in all of them wood was the fuel employed.

About the beginning of the seventeenth century, a great impulse was given to English manufacturing industries by the importation of improvements from the Continent, and by the arrival of many foreign adventurers who brought with them a knowledge of numerous appliances which, though long known on the Continent, had not yet been introduced into England. Among these improvements were new forms of furnaces which appear to have been introduced from Germany and Hungary by one Henry Wright about 1610, in which year a patent was granted for employing them to melt bell-metal, &c., with coal instead of wood.

In the following year a patent was solicited for newly-invented furnaces for making glass with coal, a project which occasioned great alarm to Jean Carré, a Frenchman, who had built glass-houses in Sussex and London "at his own great cost," and who entreated the Lord Secretary that the suit might not be granted. The Government, however, was anxious to promote all measures calculated to check the consumption of wood, and Carré's expostulations were of no avail.

The patent for the process of making glass with coal was purchased from the original patentees by Sir Robert Mansell, Vice-Admiral of England, in 1614-15, and immediately afterwards a Royal proclamation was issued prohibiting the manufacture of glass with wood, and also the importation of glass from abroad. King James was himself interested in Mansell's monopoly, having been promised a revenue of 1,000$l.$ per annum from it. The King at the same time was amused at his admiral taking to glass-making. He wondered, he said, "that Robin Mansell, being a seaman, whereby he had got much honour, should fall from water to tamper with fire, which are two contrary elements."

On being vested with the glass monopoly, Mansell set gallantly to work to develop the new process; but the task which he had entered upon proved no light one. He brought over skilled workmen from the Continent to assist him; but for several years all his experiments were abortive. He erected works successively at London, the Isle of Purbeck, Milford Haven, and on the Trent, without accomplishing anything beyond "melting vast sums of money in this glass business." At last, however, his indomitable perseverance was rewarded. About 1619 he tried works near Newcastle-on-Tyne which proved a success, and here the glass trade took root and flourished; the works established by Mansell being carried on uninterruptedly till the middle of the present century. They were long presided over by three families of Huguenot glass-makers, natives of Lorraine, named Henzell, Tytory, and Tyzack, some of whose descendants remain in the district at the present day.

The substitution of coal for wood in the smelting of metalliferous ores, and particularly in the manufacture of iron, was the most important as well as the most difficult industrial problem of the seventeenth century. The idea was not altogether new. As early as 1528 Cardinal Wolsey, then Bishop of Durham, projected a scheme for applying the coal from his mines on the Tyne to smelt the lead from his mines in Weardale, and had a large house and furnace built for the purpose near Gateshead-on-Tyne; but the cardinal's downfall and death occurring soon after, the enterprise was abandoned.

The subject was again mooted in the reign of Queen Elizabeth, and a patent for making iron and steel and melting lead "with earth coal, sea coal, turf, and peat," was granted to Thomas Proctor and William Peterson in 1589. The scheme, however, proved a commercial failure. There is a report relative to the making of two tons of iron by this process, at an iron-work in Yorkshire, from which it appears that the cost of this quantity amounted to two hundred marks (or 66*l.* 13*s.* 4*d.*

per ton), and so, says the reporter, "it is deere iron." And in the *hammering* of the iron they are stated to have wrought a whole month, night and day, " sondaie and other."

In the above-mentioned patent there is distinct allusion to the subjecting of the fuel to a preparatory process of coking, or *cooking*—indeed coked peat was the fuel used in the trial referred to—and immediately afterwards we find the treatment of coal in this way made the subject of a separate patent; a licence being granted in 1590 to the Dean of York " to purify pit coal and free it from its offensive smell." But some time elapsed before coked coal came to be applied in the arts.

As the scarcity of wood fuel became more and more felt, the attempts to employ coal in smelting became more frequent, and in the reign of James I. we enter upon a regular series of projects for effecting this much desired object. A patent was granted to Robert Chantrell in 1607 " to make and forge iron and steel with stone coal, sea coal, pit coal, and peat coal;" but no satisfactory results having been achieved, a new patent was granted in 1612 to Simon Sturtevant, a German, whose scheme, as described in his treatise on *Metallica*, was of a much more comprehensive character than those which had preceded it. His patent was for a term of thirty-one years, and included the making and working of iron, steel, lead, tin, copper, brass, &c., with sea coal, pit coal, earth coal, and brush fuel. The saving expected to be effected by his new processes was set down by Sturtevant at 330,000*l*. per annum. He seems to have been in no hurry to put his projects into execution, in consequence of which, and the fact of his being an outlaw, the patent was cancelled at the end of a year, and a new grant made to John Rovenzon, who had been one of his associates in the enterprise.

But though Rovenzon had secured the patent he appears to have been able to accomplish nothing, and for this reason, after the expiration of some years, another grant was made in 1620 to a company consisting of Sir William St. John, Sir Giles Mompesson, Sir George Ayloffe, knights; Lewis Powell, Walter Vaughan, John Pruthero, and Henry Vaughan, esquires; Henry Stubbs, gentleman, and Hugh Grundy, for "charking" sea coal, pit coal, stone coal, turf, peat, &c., and employing the same for smelting ores and manufacturing metals, and other purposes. The project originated with Grundy, and referred specially to the making of coke by a process invented by him; but notwithstanding the powerful support which he obtained, this enterprise, like the preceding ones, proved a failure, so far as the smelting of minerals was concerned.

One of the chief obstacles to success in the early attempts to smelt with coal, or coke, seems to have been the want of a sufficiently powerful blast. With charcoal fuel a very light blast sufficed. Thus the lead smelters of Derbyshire employed no artificial means to produce a blast, but built their boles, or furnaces, on lofty situations exposed to the west wind, and lighted up their fires when this wind began to blow. Rovenzon (doubtless following Sturtevant's example) employed a wind furnace "to save the charge of bellows." Whether he kept the ore and fuel separate does not appear; by his patent he was at liberty to use furnaces either with or without a division. Grundy and his partners, on the other hand, were restricted to the use of common furnaces in which the fuel and ore were mixed up together; but regarding their experiments, we only know that nothing came out of them.

The first to achieve some measure of success in smelting with coal was Dud Dudley. His efforts were directed exclusively to the manufacture of iron. Dud Dudley was a natural son of Edward, Lord Dudley, of Dudley Castle, Staffordshire. As a boy he took great delight in observing the various processes pursued in the manufacture of iron at his father's ironworks, and thus early acquired some practical acquaintance with the subject. In 1619 Dudley, then twenty years of age, was brought from Baliol College, Oxford, to manage an iron furnace and two forges, belonging to his father, in Pesnet Chase, Worcestershire. When he entered upon the charge of the works charcoal fuel alone was used, but the supply being scanty, and coal abounding in the immediate neighbourhood of the works, notwithstanding his knowledge of the failures which had already attended the attempts of others, he resolved to try for himself whether coal might not be substituted for charcoal.

Having made some alterations in his furnace, Dudley found at his first trial that he could make iron profitably with coal fuel. A second trial was made with the like result; and immediately afterwards he wrote to his father announcing the success of his experiments, and desiring him to obtain a patent for the process. This Lord Dudley forthwith proceeded to do, and a patent, dated 21st February, 1621, "for melting iron ore, making bar iron, &c., with coal, in furnaces, with bellows," was taken out in the name of Lord Dudley himself.

The discovery which Dud Dudley had made, though it has given him an enduring name in the annals of iron smelting, proved disastrous to his personal fortunes and peace of mind. The charcoal ironmasters were bitterly opposed to the new process, and declared the iron manufactured by it to be unfit for use. Even the forces of nature seemed to conspire against him; within a year after the patent was obtained his works were "ruinated" by an extraordinary flood, long afterwards known as "the great May-day flood"—an event which occasioned great joy to the rival ironmasters. Dudley, however, set about repairing his works and recommenced making iron; but so loud were the complaints of its bad quality that he was commanded by King

James "with all speed possible, to send all sorts of bar iron up to the Tower of London, fit for making muskets, carbines, and iron for great bolts fit for shipping; which iron," says Dudley, "being so tried by artists and smiths, the ironmasters and ironmongers were all silenced until the 21st of King James" (1623-4 A.D.). At this time an endeavour was made to get the patent suppressed as a monopoly, but so much importance was attached to the process that it was specially exempted in the general revocation of monopolies which then took place, though the term of the patent was limited to fourteen years. Dudley now went on with his invention cheerfully, but his prosperity was of short duration. For some reason or other his works were taken from him. He does not explain the circumstances, merely intimating that he was ousted of his works and inventions "by the ironmasters and others wrongfully, over long to relate."

Dudley now removed into Staffordshire and started afresh at Himley Furnace, but here he was crippled by the want of a forge, which compelled him to sell his pig-iron to the charcoal ironmasters, who, he tells us, did him much harm by disparaging its quality. This furnace, however, being soon afterwards rented out to charcoal ironmasters, Dudley's operations were again interrupted.

Up till this time the new process had not been much of a success. It had hitherto been carried on in furnaces originally built for smelting with charcoal. Dudley had in consequence been obliged to use very light charges, and had only been able to produce iron at the rate of three tons per week, or about a third of the quantity that could be run in the ordinary way. He now proceeded to erect a new large furnace at Hasco Bridge, Staffordshire, after his own design. This furnace was twenty-seven feet square, and was provided with extra-large bellows. With his improved arrangements he succeeded in making seven tons of iron per week, "the greatest quantity of pit coal iron that ever yet was made in Britain." Near the same place Dudley found the "Staffordshire Thick Coal," and ironstone underneath it, which he proceeded to open out and work. His affairs were now beginning to assume a more prosperous aspect, but his enemies soon found him out. The coal works were no sooner begun than he was forcibly ejected from them, "and the bellows of his new furnace and invention by riotous persons cut in pieces; so that with law-suits and riots being wearied and disabled" he was compelled to desist from his operations, and from this time he becomes lost to sight for a number of years.

In the meantime new schemes for smelting with coal continued to be brought forward. A patent for making iron with coal was granted to William Astell, John Copley, and Francis Croft, in 1627, but they succeeded no better than their predecessors. The matter was next taken up by the learned and ingenious

Dr. Jorden, of Bath, who, in 1632, obtained a patent for melting tin, iron, lead, and copper with pit coal, peat, and turf. Dr. Jorden's efforts were specially directed to the smelting of tin with coal, and though he failed to bring his scheme to a successful issue, he remained confident of its ultimate accomplishment.

About this time considerable attention began to be paid to the charring, or coking, of coal, not only in connection with the smelting experiments which were going on, but with a view to its employment for other purposes as well. In 1627 a patent was granted to Sir John Hacket, and one Octavius de Strada (who two years before had been making attempts to smelt with coal in Hainault), for a method of rendering sea coal and pit coal as useful as charcoal, for burning in houses, without offence by the smell or smoke. A few years afterwards (1633) another patent was granted to a company consising of Sir Abraham Williams, John Gaspar van Wolfen, Edward Hanchett, Amadis van Wolfen, Walter Williams, Henry Regnolds, John Brown, and Gaspar Frederick van Wolfen, for a new way of "charking" sea coal and other earth coal, and for preparing, dressing, and qualifying them so as to make them fit for the melting and making of iron and other metals, and many other good uses.

During the next three or four years some eight or nine patents were granted for the employment of smokeless preparations of coal; and though the application of coke to the smelting of minerals was not accomplished till long afterwards, it came into use at this time for several other purposes, particularly for making malt. Houghton tells us that up till about 1640 the malt was made with straw fuel in Derbyshire, but that it then came to be made with coke, which occasioned an improvement in the quality of the brewings "and brought about that alteration which all England admired."

A little later an attempt to substitute coke for coal in house fires was made by Sir John Winter. The project is referred to by Evelyn in his diary under date 11th July, 1656, in the following terms:—

"Came home by Greenwich Ferry, where I saw Sir John Winter's new project of charring sea-coale to burne out the sulphure and render it sweete. He did it by burning the coals in such earthen pots as the glasse-men mealt their mettal, so firing them without consuming them, using a barr of yron in each crucible or pot, which barr has a hook at one end, that so the coales being mealted in a furnace with other crude sea-coals under them, may be drawn out of the pots sticking to the yron, whence they are beaten off in greate halfe-exhausted cinders, which being rekindled make a cleare pleasant chamber fire, deprived of their sulphur and arsenic malignity. What success it may have, time will discover."

Sir John sent some of his "cooked coal," together with a new-fashioned grate, to several great men for a trial, but his project did not succeed.

No sooner had Dr. Jorden failed in his attempts to

smelt with coal than the matter was taken up by others. A patent for the purpose was granted, in 1636, to Sir Philibert Vernat, a Dutchman; and another, in 1637, to Vernat and Captain Whitmore. In the following year Dud Dudley again came to the front, and in conjunction with three partners obtained a patent of a more comprehensive character than his previous one, viz., to smelt all kinds of minerals with coal. But he was opposed by Vernat and Whitmore, and before anything had been effected the civil wars came on, and for a period of thirteen years no further trials were made.

In 1651, when the country had become settled again, Dudley made another attempt to set up an ironwork near Bristol. He entered into partnership with Walter Stevens, a linen-draper, and John Ston, a merchant, of Bristol. But after 700*l.* had been expended upon the works, a difference occurred between Dudley and his partners, which involved him in another law-suit, and led to the collapse of the scheme.

In the same year a project to smelt iron with raw coal was set on foot by Captain Jeremy Buck, who obtained at Act of Parliament for the purpose. Cromwell and many of his officers, and many doctors of physic, and merchants, were partners in the enterprise. They appear to have pursued a course similar to Rovenzon, employing wind-furnaces and keeping the ore and fuel separate. Several furnaces were built at great cost in the Forest of Dean. One Edward

Dagney, an Italian, and an ingenious glass-maker, of Bristol, made many pots of glass-house clay for them; but they all broke and failed. The partners importuned Dudley to visit their works, and he pronounced it impossible to make iron with coal in pots to profit; but so confident were they of success that they persevered in their own plan and invited Dudley to come back again "to see it effected." The second attempt, however, failed like the first. Afterwards Buck and his partners removed from the Forest of Dean to Bristol, where they erected new works; but here having no better success than before they finally desisted in 1656.

In the following year the matter was taken up by Captain John Copley, who obtained a patent from Cromwell. Copley built a blast-furnace at the coal-works near Bristol, and employed engineers to make his bellows to blow; but after an expenditure of several hundred pounds it was found that the bellows would not work. Dudley (who appears to have resided at Bristol at this time) went to see the works, and told Copley, who was an old acquaintance, that even if his bellows could blow he feared he could not smelt iron with coal. Dudley, moreover, without the help of any engine, made the bellows to be blown "feisibly" by manual labour; but his prophecy appears to have proved correct, as Copley soon abandoned the scheme and removed from the neighbourhood.

Immediately upon the arrival of Charles II. in England we find Dudley petitioning to be restored to his estate (which he had forfeited as a royalist), and to his patent for making iron with coal. But he was only one among a crowd of supplicants for Royal favour. He failed to procure a patent; and Colonel Proger, who applied for a patent for the same purpose in the following year, seems to have fared no better.

Notwithstanding the many failures which had attended the attempts to substitute coal for wood in the smelting of minerals up to this time, individuals were not wanting who still continued to hope and expect that this desideratum would eventually be accomplished. "It is to be hoped," wrote Dr. Fuller, in 1662, "that a way may be found out to charke sea coal in such manner as to render it useful for the making of iron. All things are not found out in one age, as reserved for future discovery: and that perchance may be easy for the next, which seems impossible to this generation."

Even as late as 1686 the problem still remained unsolved. Dr. Plot, writing at this time, gives an account of an attempt made in Staffordshire a few years before by Dr. Frederick de Blewstone, a German, to smelt iron with raw coal. He built his furnace at Wednesbury, "so ingeniously contrived (that only the flame of the coal should come to the ore, with several other conveniences) that many were of opinion he would succeed in it. But experience, that great baffler of speculation, showed it would not be ; the sulphureous vitriolic steams that issue from the *pyrites* which frequently, if not always, accompanies pit coal ascending with the flame and poisoning the ore."

But success was now near at hand. In 1692 a company was incorporated for smelting lead with coal. Leigh tells us in his *Natural History of Lancashire* that shortly before 1700 iron was being made "by means of cakes of pit coal" (*i.e.* coke). And at nearly the same time coal was successfully applied to the smelting of both tin and copper. So that as the general introduction of coal for domestic purposes was the distinguishing feature of the coal trade at the close of the sixteenth century, its successful application to the smelting of metalliferous ores may be regarded as marking another epoch in the use of coal at the close of the seventeenth century.

CHAPTER VI.

INCREASE OF MINING DIFFICULTIES.—IMPROVEMENTS IN MINING APPLIANCES.—INVENTION OF RAILWAYS.

"Mens agitat molem."

THE miners, no less than the smelters, had their difficulties during the seventeenth century, but of a totally different kind; for while the latter were suffering from too little fire, the former were embarrassed by too much water. So long as the demand for coal was small, and supplies were obtainable from shallow mines above the level of free-drainage, the mining of coal had been comparatively easy. But about the beginning of the seventeenth century, this happy state of matters was coming to an end. A great demand for coal had sprung up. Much of the most easily available coal had already been exhausted. To carry the workings down into the region below the level of free-drainage was at this time deemed impracticable. To procure sufficient coal from the previous sources was impossible. Hence the exhaustion of the coal supply was considered to be already within sight. In 1610, Sir George Selby informed Parliament that the coal mines at Newcastle would not last for the term of their leases of twenty-one years.

It was at this period, when the coal trade was supposed to be hastening to its close, that the real work of mining coal only began. By the employment of machinery for raising the water from the mines, which now became general, the horizon of mining operations was indefinitely extended. But the effectual drainage of the mines was a work of the greatest difficulty, as is sufficiently evidenced by the innumerable patents which were taken out during the course of the century for machines invented for the purpose. Indeed the seventeenth century may not inaptly be termed the *wet period* of coal mining.

The improvements introduced into coal mining at this time were due to a considerable extent to adventurers, who were attracted into the coal trade by the increased importance now attaching to it, and by the advance in the value of coal. Among these a gentleman named Beamont, or Beaumont, makes a prominent figure, many new and ingenious contrivances being introduced by him into the Newcastle-on-Tyne district. The earliest historian of Newcastle, writing in 1649, refers to this matter in the following terms:—

"Some south gentlemen have upon great hope of benefit come into this country (*i.e.* district) to hazard their monies in coal pits. Master Beamont, a gentleman of great ingenuity and rare parts, adventured into our mines with his thirty thousand pounds; who brought with him many rare engines not known then in these parts: as the art to bore with iron rods to try the deepness and thickness of the coal; rare engines to draw water out of the pits; waggons with one horse to carry down coals from the pits to the staiths at the river, &c. Within few years he consumed all his money and rode home upon his light horse."

It has usually been supposed that the arrival of Beamont with his "rare engines" took place shortly before the above was written, but it has recently been pointed out by Mr. Clephan, of Newcastle, that this event must have occurred considerably earlier, in fact near the commencement of the century, inasmuch as a payment is recorded in the household books of Naworth Castle for "a set of boring rods bought at Newcastle," in July, 1618. Regarding this ingenious individual, whose mining venture, though fraught with benefit to the Newcastle-on-Tyne district, proved disastrous to himself, we have no further information. Where he obtained his superior knowledge of mining machinery we can only conjecture. But as we find the engines commonly used for raising water from the coal mines during the seventeenth century to have been such as had been known and used in the metalliferous mines of the Continent during the previous century, it is probable that he obtained some of his ideas at least directly or indirectly from this source. He appears to have been the discoverer of a new seam of coal which bears the name of the "Beaumont" or "Engine seam" to this day.

Among the engines applied to raise water from the coal mines at this time were several forms of chain pumps. One of these consisted of a chain to which circular iron plates were attached at short intervals. These plates in ascending travelled through a tube which they exactly fitted, like so many pistons, thus bearing the water before them. Sometimes a bunch of rags was substituted for plates, when it took the name of the "rag-and-chain pump."

A more important engine was the chain of buckets, or Egyptian wheel, a machine which had been used in the East for ages for drawing water from deep wells. The construction of this machine resembled that of the modern dredger of which it was the prototype.

An Egyptian wheel was fitted up, about or before the year 1600, by Sir George Bruce, to re-open the colliery of Culross, in Perthshire, which had been abandoned for some time. Sir George was famed for his knowledge and great skill in machinery, "such like," it is stated, "as no other man has in these days," and he made his colliery at Culross the wonder of the district, the workings being carried to a distance of a mile underneath the Frith of Forth. The colliery had two pits, or shafts, one of which was situated in a little artificial island on the fore-shore near low-water mark. The other pit was on the edge of the shore, and here was placed the engine which drew the water from the mine. It was driven by three horses, and consisted of an endless chain with thirty-six buckets attached to it, of which eighteen were continually descending empty, and eighteen ascending full of water. The buckets filled themselves in the well at the bottom of the pit, and emptied themselves into a trough at the top as they passed over the axle-tree.

Tradition records that King James paid a visit to Sir George Bruce in 1617, and went to see his wonderful colliery. The royal party entered the mine by the shaft on the land, and in returning were brought up the other shaft on the island. The tide happened to be high at the time, and the King, not knowing the peculiar arrangement of the mine, on arriving at the top and seeing himself surrounded by the waves, at once suspected a plot on his life, and shouted "Treason!" His host, however, instantly explained the matter, pointing to a beautiful pinnace waiting to take the party on shore, and the King's equanimity was restored.

In the latter part of the seventeenth century chain pumps driven by water-wheels were employed to drain the principal collieries in the North of England, viz., Heaton, Jesmond, and Ravensworth collieries, on the Tyne, and Lumley Colliery on the Wear. In 1672 some of these collieries had attained to the depth of forty fathoms. The water, however, was not raised from this depth in one lift, but in several stages. Thus at Ravensworth Colliery, the property of Sir Thomas Liddell, the water engines of which were considered to be the most remarkable in the North of England at this time, the total depth was divided into three stages. The water was raised each stage by means of a separate engine and pit. Three water-wheels were required, all driven by the same stream; one being placed on high pillars, the second on the surface of the ground, and the third under the surface. The power to work the second and third stages was transmitted from the water-wheels by means of vertical shafting and wheel-work placed in the respective pits.

At Lumley Colliery on the Wear, at the same period, there were two of these engines (one of three stories, and the other of two), which served to drain all the pits within a radius of two or three miles.

Chain and bucket engines driven by water-wheels were also commonly employed to drain the collieries in the east of Scotland at this time. Many large artificial ponds were constructed at great cost for supplying water to these machines.

Where water-power could not be had smaller engines of the same description were sometimes worked by horses, but more commonly machines similar to those employed in raising the coal were applied to raise the water in barrels. The earliest form of horse engine, or "gin," employed for raising both coals and water, appears to have been the "cog and rung gin," which was obviously only a windlass adapted to be worked by horses, instead of by manual labour, by the addition of a wheel and pinion arrangement. The horse travelled round the pit mouth pulling a lever attached to a vertical shaft, and the cogs, or teeth, of a horizontal wheel on this shaft, worked in the rungs, or spokes, of a small pinion on the windlass or drum shaft, thus making it to revolve in the required direction.

Recourse was still had to adits, or water-levels, to drain off the water from mines situated on high ground, and many long tunnels were driven for this purpose, at great cost, in the latter part of the seventeenth century. "When they are by the side of a hill," says Roger North, speaking of the Newcastle miners in 1676, "they drain by a level carried a mile underground, and cut through rock to the value of 5,000*l*. or 6,000*l*." The same writer mentions among the "strange histories" of the Newcastle coal works, an attempt made by Sir Walter Blackett to cut into a hill for purposes of drainage which was foiled by reason of the drift penetrating a bed of soft clay. Sir Walter, he tells us, "conquered all difficulties of stone and the like till he came to clay, and that was too hard for him, for no means of timber or walls would assist, but all was crowded together.[1] In this work he lost 20,000*l*."

---

[1] The difficulty of penetrating horizontally through clay when hard rock can be perforated with comparative ease has long been subject of remark. Pliny was amused at the inability of the Spanish miners to accomplish it.

In other parts of the kingdom in like manner numbers of long water-levels were driven at this period. The increasing length of the levels rendered it necessary to introduce modifications in the " Laws and Customs of the miners in the Forest of Dean." Here in ancient times the bounds of a mine had been fixed at the distance to which the miner could throw the rubbish from his pit—an arrangement which speaks of a highly primitive stage of mining. Availing themselves of this ancient custom, when an adit was driven other miners came and sunk pits so near to it as to rob the drivers of the adit of much of the benefit of their labour. It was therefore enacted by the "Mine Law Court," in 1678, that no miner might sink a pit within one hundred yards of an adit belonging to another man without his consent. This distance was extended in 1692 to three hundred yards, and subsequently to one thousand yards.

When it became necessary for the miners to seek for coal at greater depths than formerly, it was of the utmost consequence that they should obtain information regarding the character of the strata beneath; whether any valuable coal existed, and at what depth; or otherwise their shafts might be sunk, and all their time and labour expended in vain. To effect this *bore-rods* were invented, an invaluable apparatus to which allusion has already been made in connection with its introduction into the Newcastle-on-Tyne district by Beamont.

By means of this ingenious contrivance holes a few inches in diameter can be drilled to the depth of hundreds of feet; samples of the strata passed through brought up; and the depth, thickness, and quality of coal seams ascertained at comparatively small cost.

This useful art was already widely known early in the seventeenth century. It is alluded to, though in somewhat vague terms, in Rovenzon's *Metallica*, published in 1613. Bore-rods, as we have seen, were purchased at Newcastle-on-Tyne in 1618, by Lord William Howard, of Naworth Castle; and ten years later we find the same nobleman sending a borer to the Forest of Dean, to assist his son-in-law, Sir John Winter, in searching for coal there. In Warwickshire, in 1623, the lessees of Bedworth coal-mines were prohibited from boring any holes which might endanger adjoining mines by flooding them with water let down from the surface; and in 1639 a series of borings were made by one Thomas Wake in the neighbourhood of Leeds. Borers of this name continued to practise the art long subsequently in the Newcastle-on-Tyne district.

References to boring operations are frequent during the seventeenth century. They sometimes gave rise to unexpected discoveries, as in Cheshire, where in 1670 a borer failed to find coal which he was searching for, but discovered the existence of valuable deposits of rock salt.

The application of gunpowder to the blasting of rocks appears to belong to the same period as the invention of the boring apparatus. It was practised to some extent in the metalliferous mines of Germany as early as 1613, but did not come into use in England till a later period. A method of blasting with gunpowder was described in the *Philosophical Transactions* in 1665. The first application of the process in England was at the Ecton Hill copper-mines, in Staffordshire, about this time, where it was doubtless introduced by the German miners employed. It came into use in the lead mines of the Mendip Hills, Somersetshire, about 1683, up to which time *fire-setting*[1] had been the only means known there for breaking up hard rock. Soon afterwards it began to be practised in the metalliferous mines of other districts, but for a long period the methods of stemming or plugging the shot holes appear to have been very imperfect, and the operation of firing the charge difficult and dangerous.[2] There is no mention of the use of gunpowder in coal mines till a considerably later period.

---

[1] The application of fire and vinegar to break up rock by expansion and contraction was a very ancient process. It was employed by Hannibal in making a road for his army across the Alps; the work being doubtless executed by his Spanish miners.

[2] At a much later period (1758) we hear of an explosion of fire-damp being caused in a shaft at Middleton Colliery, near Leeds, sixty yards deep, by the miners throwing down fire from the top to ignite a charge of gunpowder.

The event, however, to which the greatest general interest attaches in connection with the coal industry at this period is the invention of *railways*. Unfortunately no historian has left us an account of the first introduction of this invention, which from a humble beginning has risen to such extraordinary importance. Neither the date of its first application, nor the name of the inventor with whom the happy thought of the wheel and rail adapted to each other originated, have been handed down to us. Even the district where railways first came into use is not altogether certain. We know, however, that they were invented for the conveyance of coal from the pits to the place of shipment, and that they were in use shortly after the middle of the seventeenth century in the North of England, and in Shropshire about the same time. They were for a long period constructed entirely of wood, iron being then a material much too scarce and costly to employ for such a purpose.

So long as the demand for coal was limited, and the trade moderate in extent, the means employed for the conveyance of ordinary articles had also sufficed for the conveyance of coal. Up till the year 1600 no improvement in this direction had taken place at the Newcastle collieries. A record of this date in the books of the Hostmen's Company sets forth that "from time out of mind it hath been accustomed that all coal wains did usually carry and bring eight bolls of coals to the staiths upon the river of Tyne"; and the only other means of conveyance referred to is "small panniers holding two or three pecks apiece." The first notice of any attempts to effect improvements occurs in the account of the novelties introduced into the north by Beamont, among which, as we have seen, were "waggons with one horse to carry down coals from the pits to the staiths." It has been supposed that this passage implies the use of railways, and that they were consequently introduced by Beamont; but if so it is remarkable that no allusion is made to the circumstance either in this or in another passage by the same writer where, in speaking of the large population supported by the trade in coals, he tells us that "many live by conveying them in waggons and wains to the river Tyne." In the absence of direct evidence it is therefore uncertain whether railways had come into use in the north previous to the middle of the seventeenth century, but immediately after this period we meet with notices of them. Thus Mr. T. J. Taylor cites a document, dated 1660, relating to the sale, among other things, of certain "wood or timber laid upon trenches, bridges, and *waggon-ways*, or unlaid upon the same." It was some time after this, however, before they came much into use.

Railways and waggons appear to have begun to be used in leading coals from Sir Thomas Liddell's colliery at Ravensworth to Team Staith in 1671. A few years later the new method of conveyance attracted the attention of Roger North, who, writing in 1676, refers to the subject in the following terms :—

"Another thing that is remarkable [at the Newcastle collieries] is their way-leaves, for when men have pieces of ground between the colliery and the river, they sell leave to lead coals over their ground, and so dear that the owner of a rood of ground will expect 20*l.* per annum for this leave. The manner of the carriage is by laying rails of timber from the colliery down to the river, exactly straight and parallel, and bulky carts are made with four rowlets fitting these rails, whereby the carriage is so easy that one horse will draw down four or five chaldrons of coals, and is an immense benefit to coal merchants."

This account seems to indicate a considerable improvement upon the "waggons with one horse" above referred to; the improvement being probably due to the invention of the railway in the interim.

Before railways came into use a prodigious number of carts and wains were required to carry the produce of the Newcastle collieries to the shipping places on the Tyne. The collieries of Kenton and Benwell each employed from four to five hundred; and in 1690, Whickham Colliery had no fewer than six hundred wains in use leading coals to the river.

The Wear district soon followed the example of the Tyne district in the adoption of railways; the new method of conveyance being first applied there, in 1693, by Thomas Allan, Esq., of Newcastle-on-Tyne, the proprietor of Allan's Flatts Colliery, near Chester-le-Street.

The history of the early use of railways in the coalfields of the South-west is even more obscure than in the case of the North of England. When they first came to be employed in Shropshire we have been unable to discover. Professor Pepper, in his *Play Book of Metals*, speaks of Coalbrookdale as being "celebrated as the place where railroads formed of wood were first used in the year 1620 and 1650," but without adducing any evidence in support of the statement.

They were introduced into South Wales by the ingenious Sir Humphry Mackworth, who had one already constructed at his colliery at Neath, in Glamorganshire, in 1698. This railway, after being about eight years in use, was declared by the grand jury at Cardiff to be *a nuisance*, and a portion of it crossing the highway between Cardiff and Neath was torn up and the rails cut in pieces. In some evidence brought forward (about 1706) to rebut the presentment of the Cardiff jury, it is set forth that—

"These waggon-ways are very common and frequently made use of about Newcastle, and also at Broseley, Benthal, and other places in Shropshire, and are so far from being nuisances that they have ever been esteemed very useful to preserve the roads, which would be otherwise made very bad and deep by the carriage of coal in common waggons and carts."

F

Not only had Sir Humphry Mackworth introduced the most improved methods of conveyance for his coal, but a number of other novelties were to be found at his collieries and copper-works at Neath. As early as 1698 he was employing coal in the smelting of copper. He also had several schemes for enlisting the force of the wind in his service, and had invented "new sailing waggons for the cheap carriage of his coal to the water-side, whereby one horse does the work of ten at all times, but when any wind is stirring one man and a small sail does the work of twenty." He had in like manner set up "sailing engines," or wind-mills, for other purposes. As Yalden says of him in his poem :—

"The winds, thy slaves, their useful succour join,
Convey thy ore, and labour at thy mine."

But among the various productions of the genius of Sir Humphry Mackworth, vastly the most important in a mining point of view was "his new method of coffering out the water from his shafts and sinking-pits, and thereby preventing the charges of water-engines." Waller tells us that by this means Sir Humphry succeeded in recovering a large vein of coal which had been in vain attempted by other artists. This seems to be the earliest notice we have of the invaluable process of damming out water from coal-pits by means of a water-tight lining, termed in the North of England *tubbing,* from the circumstance of its having originally consisted of a frame of wooden staves like the sides of a tub. This excellent invention, already important at this time as the shafts were becoming deeper, has become infinitely more so at the present day. Indeed, without a system of keeping the water out of the shafts in this way, the working of deep seams of coal lying under very wet strata would in many cases be altogether impracticable.

CHAPTER VII.

NOXIOUS GASES PREVALENT IN THE MINES.—ACCIDENTS OCCASIONED THEREBY.—SMALL EXPLOSIONS OF FIRE-DAMP BECOME FREQUENT.

> "And oft a chilling damp or unctuous mist,
> Loosed from the crumbling caverns, issues forth,
> Stopping the springs of life . . . .
> . . . . . . To cure this ill
> A philosophic art is used to drain
> The foul imprison'd air, and in its place
> Purer convey." —JAGO.

WHILST water was the chief enemy with which the miners had to contend during the era under consideration, it was not the only one. As the mine workings receded further and further from the surface, the supply of air arising from natural ventilation gradually ran short, and noxious gases became a source of increasing trouble and danger.

During the middle ages phenomena connected with the atmosphere of mines which were beyond the comprehension of the miners were usually ascribed to the supernatural agency of fairies and goblins, whose opposition was to be overcome by means of fasting and prayer. Before the light of scientific investigation, however, these ignorant and superstitious notions began to give way. The subterranean spirits vanished into air, or rather became metamorphosed into noxious gases. The apparently altogether capricious phenomena were demonstrated to be occasioned by purely natural causes, and ventilation was found to produce a more effective exorcism than the methods previously adopted. During the seventeenth century nearly all mines were more or less subject either to "choke-damp" or suffocating gas, or to the still more perilous "fire-damp" or explosive gas.

Of these *choke-damp* was at this time the most common, and was most troublesome in mines where fires had existed, or where fire-setting was resorted to for splitting the rocks, and in dry mines where there was no laving, pumping, or drawing of water to set the air in motion. On account of this gas some mines could not be worked when the wind blew from certain quarters, and hence it was said in these days that a prudent collier "minds the wind." Before the miners proceeded to work in pits where this gas was suspected to be present, it was customary to try the air by first lowering a dog down the shaft, which began to howl as soon as it entered the choke-damp, or by lowering down a light, which became extinguished if the gas were present.

The usual method of procuring larger supplies of air at this time, was to sink air-shafts for the purpose. At Cheadle, in North Staffordshire, however, where fire-setting was practised, the additional expedient of placing a fire-lamp, or grate full of burning coals, in the air-shaft to produce a circulation of air through the workings to clear away the smoke and gases arising from these fires, was resorted to previous to 1686—an early example of artificial ventilation by means of fire placed in the mine.

An accident which was probably due to the presence of this gas occurred in the year 1662, when seven or eight men and one woman were suffocated through their going into an old working, or waste, in Lord Sinclair's colliery at Dysart, in Fifeshire.[1]

Though *fire-damp*, or explosive gas, is the peculiar scourge of deep coal-mines, it has in many instances been met with in dangerous quantity at very little depth. In some cases it has even been known to come quite up to the surface, as in the famous "burning well" in Lancashire, once the wonder of the Wigan

---

[1] The method of recovering asphyxiated colliers at this period was curious. "The ordinary remedy," we are told, "is to dig a hole in the earth, and lay them on their bellies, with their mouths in it; if that fail, they tun them full of good ale; but if that fail, they conclude them desperate."

neighbourhood, where the gas boiled up through the water, and could be ignited and made to burn on the top of it.[1]

In the early part of the seventeenth century this gas had already commenced to claim its victims. Perhaps one of the first allusions to an accident from this cause is that contained in the register of St. Mary's church, Gateshead-on-Tyne, where, under date 14th October, 1621, is recorded the interment of "Richard Backas, *burn'd in a pit.*"

We next hear of fire-damp annoying the miners at the ancient colliery of Mostyn, on the estuary of the Dee, where it began to be met with about 1640. At this period a seam of coal fifteen feet thick was sunk to at a depth of twenty or thirty fathoms. When the coal was first found it was extremely full of water, but as the water drained off and the excavations receded from the shaft, thereby causing the ventilation to become weaker, fire-damp began to appear. At first the workmen made sport of it, till one morning as a collier entered his working place, where the gas happened to be present in stronger force than usual, it exploded at his candle and knocked him down, singeing all his hair and clothes, and disabling him from working for a while.

After receiving a few warnings of this kind, the

---

[1] Another burning well is stated to have existed at Broseley, in Shropshire.

miners deemed it necessary to adopt measures of precaution, and for this purpose they selected one of their number, more resolute than the rest, to go down a while before them every morning, to set fire to and explode all the small accumulations of gas. Covering himself with sackcloth saturated with water, this man (termed the *fireman*) advanced towards the place where the fire-damp existed, and creeping on his belly, held a long pole before him with one or more lighted candles at its end. This ignited the fire-damp and produced an explosion more or less violent according to the quantity of gas accumulated. As the flame ran along the roof the fireman lay flat on his belly till it passed over him. When the operations of the fireman had been completed the rest of the colliers entered the mine, and the motion of the air caused by their working prevented the gas from collecting during the day. After the works had been more fully opened out, the fire-damp ceased to annoy the miners at Mostyn for a long period.

As the seventeenth century advanced, difficulties with fire-damp became great and general. It appears to have been about 1675 that explosions first began to become alarmingly violent. At this period they did not yet occasion much loss of life, but scorched and maimed the colliers, and frequently issued with such force out of the mouth of the pit as to blow away the winding-drum placed over it.

About this time numerous explosions occurred in

different parts of the kingdom. One happened at a pit in Hasleberg-hills, by which a collier had his arms and legs broken and his body all distorted. In the summer of 1675 a pit at Wingersworth, near Chesterfield, fired four times within a few weeks, scorching and otherwise injuring a collier each time. The pit was about fifteen yards deep. One of the blasts shot off the windlass at the mouth of the pit, and carried small coals and rubbish to a considerable height into the air.

In the same year the miners at Mostyn commenced to open out a new seam of coal, which had been discovered lying twenty yards below the one already mentioned, when the fire-damp became a source of much greater difficulty than before. On the 3rd of February, 1675-6, it gave rise to an explosion of great fierceness, a graphic account of which, written by Mr. Roger Mostyn, is preserved in the *Philosophical Transactions*. One man was shot right out of the pit-mouth, and the winding-drum at the top of the pit, weighing 1,000 lbs., was blown off and torn in pieces.

It is evident from the observations of Roger North that explosions were already well known in the North of England collieries in 1676. With reference to noxious gases in the mines, he tells us that—

"Damps or foul air kill insensibly; sinking another pit that the air may not stagnate is an infallible remedy. They are most affected in very hot weather. An infallible trial is by a dog, and the candles show it. They seem to be heavy sulphurous airs, not fit to breathe, and I have heard some say that they would sometimes lie in the midst of a shaft and the bottom be clear. The flame of a candle will not kindle them so soon as the snuff, but they have been kindled by the striking fire with a tool.[1] The blast is mighty violent, but men have been saved by lying flat on their bellies."

At the same period fire-damp had become formidable in the collieries near Mendip Hills, in Somersetshire. An account written in 1681 states that "many men of late years have been there killed, many others maimed and burnt; some have been blown up at the works' mouth, the turn-beam which hangs over the shaft has been thrown off its frame by the force of it."

In the collieries of Scotland fire-damp was more rare, but was not unknown. The trouble which it occasioned was assigned as one of the causes for abandoning a colliery on the Frith of Forth previous to 1672.

During the seventeenth century many under-ground fires occurred, particularly in Staffordshire, where they were so common as to excite comparatively little anxiety. These fires were sometimes attributed to the malice or carelessness of the colliers; but the liability of some coals to ignite spontaneously was now well known. Fires from this cause had occurred above-ground also, both

---

[1] Another writer of this period mentions that fire-damp had been kindled in some places "by the motion of the sled in which they draw their coals."

on the staiths at Newcastle and on the wharves at London. Coals containing pyrites (termed metal coals) were peculiarly liable to ignition in this way. Dr. Power mentions an instance which occurred at Ealand, in Yorkshire, where a person had collected many cart-loads of this pyrites for some private purpose of his own. The roof of the place where they were stored being faulty and admitting rain-water to fall copiously in among them, they began to smoke and then took fire and burnt like red-hot coals, "so that the town was in an uproar about the quenching of them."

CHAPTER VIII.

INADEQUACY OF THE WATER-RAISING MACHINERY.—INVENTION OF THE STEAM-ENGINE.

> "It is a giant with one idea."
> —COLERIDGE.

IN the beginning of the eighteenth century the common depth of the mine shafts in the North of England was from twenty to thirty fathoms, but a few had attained to depths of fifty or sixty fathoms. The deeper shafts were already entering the drier region below the zone of watery strata (which usually extends to a depth varying from fifty to a hundred fathoms from the surface), where difficulties with water begin to grow less, while difficulties with fire-damp increase in magnitude. In these deeper shafts the process of tubbing out the water by means of water-tight timber frames could already be practised with considerable success; but in the great majority of cases water continued to harass or even altogether baffle the miners: sometimes preventing them from reaching the coal in spite of all their arts, or entailing a ruinous expense in carrying on the collieries, so much so as in some instances to occasion their abandonment.

The chain of buckets was soon found to be inadequate to meet the ever-increasing wants of the miners. Without water-power to drive these engines they were of little use; and even where this was available, this kind of machine was open to many serious objections. The wear and tear was excessive; between vibration of the chains and leakage, half of the contents of the buckets was spilled before they arrived at the top; water was constantly pouring down the pit like a deluge; and when a bolt broke the whole set of chains and buckets fell to the bottom with a most tremendous crash, and every bucket was splintered into a thousand pieces.

Hence a widely-felt want existed for a suitable machine to raise the water from the mines. In the year 1708 a plan was projected in Scotland for draining collieries by means of windmills and pumps, but so backward was the state of engineering art in the country that no person was known competent to put the scheme into execution except one John Young, a millwright of Montrose, who had been sent to Holland at the expense of the town to inspect the machinery there. It was suggested that if the services of this person could not be obtained advice on the matter should be sought from the *Mechanical Priest of Lancashire*. Windmills were erected at several collieries, but though they were powerful their action was found to be too intermittent; the mines being drowned and all the workmen thrown idle during long periods of calm weather.

Pumps, however, being free from many of the defects of the chains of buckets, began to be substituted for them. We find the Earl of Mar, proprietor of Alloa Collieries in Clackmannanshire, having his water-engines altered in this way in 1710, on the recommendation of Mr. George Sorocould, an eminent engineer from Derby, whom he had called in to report on this and other matters connected with the machinery at his collieries. The alteration was found to effect a great improvement.

But the points where water-power could be obtained to drain the mines were comparatively few, and windmills, as we have seen, could not be relied upon; hence in far the most cases horse-power had to be employed, the water being drawn in barrels by means of a gin of the same description as that employed in drawing the coals. This power was capable of universal application, but it was of a limited and expensive character. In some instances as many as fifty horses were employed in raising water at a single colliery. Many good mines were allowed to lie unwrought and drowned, it being found impracticable to drain them by means of any machine then known.

Captain Savery was at this time making efforts to get his "engine for raising water by fire" introduced as a mine-draining engine. In the description of his engine entitled *The Miner's Friend*, published in 1702, he expresses himself in very sanguine terms regarding the benefits which the miners might derive from its adoption, not doubting, he says, but that in a few years it would be the means of doubling, if not trebling, the importance of the mining industry. Not only was his engine to free the mines from water, but also from "damps," or noxious gases. In applying the engine in a mine it was necessary to place it in the shaft within twenty-six or twenty-eight feet of the level of the water to be raised, a circumstance which Savery proposed to take advantage of by employing the furnace and chimney of his engine to ventilate the mine.

But Savery's engine was wholly unsuited for draining mines, and he failed to induce the miners to take it up. The greatest height to which it could raise water with safety was not more than sixty or eighty feet, so that for one of the deeper mines of this period five or six engines would have been required to raise the water stage by stage.

In addition to this there was constant danger of the boiler bursting, on account of its not being provided with any kind of safety-valve. Moreover the miners in some districts were as yet afraid to introduce furnaces into their shafts, on account of the dread of their giving rise to explosions of fire-damp. Commenting on the engine for raising water by fire, which he had heard of, the author of the *Compleat Collier* (a treatise on mining in the Newcastle-on-Tyne district, published in 1708) remarks that he fears few in the northern collieries would venture to try it, "because *nature* doth generally afford us too much sulpherous matter, to bring more fire within these our deep bowels of the earth, so that we judge cool inventions of suction or force would be safest and best for this our concern, if any such could be found that would do so much better and with more expedition than what is done generally here."

It was at this juncture that the miners had put into their hands the most wonderful invention which human ingenuity had yet produced—the Newcomen steam-engine, commonly called the "atmospheric engine"; a machine capable of draining with ease the deepest mines; applicable anywhere; requiring little or no attention; so docile that its movements might be governed by the strength of a child; so powerful that it could put forth the strength of hundreds of horses; so safe that, to quote the words of a contemporary writer, "the utmost damage that can come to it, is its standing still for want of fire."

Soon after the discovery of the pressure of the atmosphere, and the invention of the air-pump, it became evident to philosophers that if a means could be devised to produce a vacuum under a piston sliding in a cylinder, the pressure of the atmosphere might be brought into play as a useful motive power. Huyghens endeavoured to effect this, about 1679, by employing gunpowder to expel the air from the cylinder. Papin, in 1690, suggested the use of steam in lieu of gunpowder, but did not get beyond the experimental stage of raising the steam in the cylinder itself by the application of fire to it. To Newcomen, of Dartmouth, in Devon, assisted by an associate named Cawley, of the same place, belongs the honour of perfecting the mechanism which had previously existed only in a rudimentary form. By supplying the cylinder with steam from a separate boiler, and adding numerous highly ingenious devices, by which the engine was made self-acting, Newcomen succeeded in inventing, about the year 1710, an engine of vast power and utility—an engine which "produced a new era in the mining and commercial interests of Britain, and as it were in an instant put every coalfield which was considered as lost within the grasp of its owner."

Newcomen applied his engine to actuate a common

lifting or suction pump. His first engine was built at a colliery near Wolverhampton, in Staffordshire, in 1712, and so rapidly was the invention adopted by the miners, that within the space of a few years engines were built in all the principal mining districts throughout the kingdom. Three were erected at collieries in the North of England about 1713—14, viz., one in the Wear district and two on the Tyne; another was built at Austhorpe, in Yorkshire, about 1714; and previous to 1720, engines had been erected at collieries in Scotland, at Whitehaven in Cumberland, in Warwickshire, and in North Wales.

The great superiority of Newcomen's engine over horses, in point of economy, is well illustrated by the account of the performance of an engine at Griff Colliery, in Warwickshire, which Dr. Desaguliers informs us "did discharge as much water as did before employ fifty horses, at an expense not less than 900*l.* a year; whereas the fire, in coals, attendance, and repairs, did never cost more than 150*l.* a year in this engine." Thus the water-charge at Griff was reduced to one-sixth of its previous amount.

But apart from the economy attending its use, the great value of the steam-engine lay in the fact that the miners now had in their possession a machine powerful enough to command the water in their deepest mines; the thing which, of all others, they were at this time most in want of.

CHAPTER IX.

STATE OF MINING AT THE COMMENCEMENT OF THE EIGHTEENTH CENTURY.—FIRST GREAT EXPLOSIONS IN THE NORTH OF ENGLAND COLLIERIES.

> "A narrow pass
> Once made, wide and more wide the gloomy cave
> Stretches its vaulted sides, by numerous hands
> Hourly extended. Some the pickaxe ply,
> Loos'ning the quarry from its native bed;
> Some heave it to th' expectant scale, that waits
> With never-ceasing motion from above
> To waft it to the light."
> —Jago.

Though the Newcastle-on-Tyne district was the great centre of the coal-mining industry, and the Tyne and Wear together exported 650,000 tons of coal annually at the commencement of the eighteenth century, the art of mining even here was still only in an elementary state.

The shafts (which in this district are invariably circular in form) were at this time made seven or eight feet in diameter, and their maximum depth was about sixty fathoms. The coals were drawn up the shafts in *corves*, or circular baskets made of hazel twigs, having a wooden *bow*, or handle, by which they were attached to the hook at the end of the rope. Each basket carried about $4\frac{1}{2}$ cwts. of coal. For the deeper pits an output of twenty-one scores of such baskets, or about ninety tons, was considered a good day's work. A gin, worked by two horses at a time, was used for raising the coals; and four shifts, or relays, of horses were required to carry on the work. The ropes were of hemp, and about three inches in circumference.

In addition to the "cog and rung gin," already mentioned, another and more commodious form of horse-engine, named the "whim gin," came into use. In this case the drum, or rope-roll, was removed from the pit mouth, and placed upon a vertical axis a short distance off; the ropes being conducted therefrom to pulleys fixed on a timber frame erected over the pit. The horse-track, or "gin-race," instead of being round the pit as formerly, was round the axis of the drum. This arrangement was a superior one in many respects. The pit mouth was left freer from obstruction; the diameter of the drum could be enlarged without inconvenience; and the number of horses applied to the levers could be increased as required.

Underground the baskets of coal were conveyed on sledges, or trams, dragged along the barrow-way by two or three persons (the barrow-men, or coal-putters), horses not having yet been introduced into the mines. In consequence of the difficulties connected with underground conveyance and ventilation, the area worked from each shaft was extremely limited; the coal lying within a radius of two hundred yards in all directions from the shaft being considered a sufficient extent to be worked by one pit.

A superior method of underground conveyance was in use at Madeley and other places in Shropshire, where access was obtained to the workings by means of "day-levels," or adits. Advantage was taken of this circumstance to employ small carriages with four wheels (of about twelve inches diameter), in which the coals were conveyed not only along the underground passages of the mines, but even to the boats lying in the Severn: a sight which the Rev. Francis Brokesby tells us, in a letter dated 1711, he had been very much pleased to see some years before.

The system of working coal in the North of England appears from time immemorial to have been to excavate only a certain portion of the seam, leaving the remainder to support the superincumbent strata. This is commonly known as the *bord and pillar* system. The "bords," or main excavations, are driven in parallel lines across the planes of cleavage of the seam (on account of the coal being worked most easily in this direction), and of a width of three, four, or five yards, according to the character of the roof of the mine. Between these bords, walls or ribs of coal are left, more or less thick according to the depth of the mine and consequent weight of the strata resting upon the coal; while narrow excavations (about two yards in width), termed "headways," are driven at intervals through the walls to connect the bords with each other for purposes of haulage and ventilation; the effect of the narrow excavations being to cut the walls into a series of pillars of a square or oblong form. In the deeper pits, at this period, it was customary to make the bords three yards wide, and the walls or ribs of coal four yards wide; so that more than one-half of the coal was permanently sacrificed to support the surface.

In Shropshire, and some other counties, a totally different method of working came into use. This consisted in removing the whole of the seam or vein of coal as the workings advanced from the shaft, the space previously occupied by the coal being partially or wholly packed or plugged up by refuse or pillars built of stones, while the roadways are preserved by means of walls of stones built on both sides. This system of working, sometimes designated "the Shropshire method," is more commonly known as the *long wall* system. It is akin to that pursued in working metalliferous veins, from which doubtless the principle was derived.

Between the extreme types of bord and pillar and long wall, many intermediate methods of working were adopted in different districts, usually with a view to meet peculiar local conditions.

At the beginning of the eighteenth century little or no improvement had been effected in the ventilation of coal-mines. Even in the North of England no artificial system of ventilation had yet been instituted, though steps were already taken to guide the air-current arising from natural ventilation into such parts of the mine as were actually in work; it being prevented from dispersing itself irregularly by means of checks termed "stoppings," which were placed in the excavated passages where necessary. But the only means employed to produce a circulation of air was to sink another pit before the workings advanced too far; "which, if happily done by the daily care, prudence, and orders of the viewer," says the author of the *Compleat Collier*, "and his drift to the new pit carried on so exactly as to hit the new shaft and supply her with air, then has he evidenced both his care and parts, and well deserved his 15s. or 20s. per week, or more, as he has pits to look after."

It was at this period in the history of coal-mining, when the pits had reached a depth of about sixty fathoms, and entered the drier region, already referred to, where the fissures which had previously been filled with water or choke-damp were now charged with fire-damp instead, that we begin to meet with accounts of great colliery explosions.

The first of these calamities in the collieries on the Tyne occurred in a pit near Gateshead, on the 3rd or 4th of October, 1705, and occasioned the loss of over thirty lives. The pit was upwards of sixty fathoms in depth, yet so fierce was the blast that six individuals (including one woman) are stated to have been blown out of its mouth. The parish register of Gateshead contains a record of the interments of the unhappy victims of this early explosion, the melancholy list being headed by the words, "These were slain in a coal-pit in the Stony Flat, which did fire."

Only a few years later the mining community in the north was startled by a still more dreadful explosion at Fatfield Colliery, near Chester-le-Street, on the river Wear. This accident occurred at three o'clock in the morning on the 18th of August, 1708. The fire discharged itself at the mouths of three shafts "with as great a noise as the firing of cannons, or the loudest claps of thunder," and sixty-nine persons were instantly destroyed. Three persons, viz. two men and one woman, were blown out of a shaft fifty-seven fathoms deep, and carried a considerable distance from its mouth. An account of this explosion was communicated to the Royal Society at the time, and published in the *Philosophical*

Transactions. After describing the dangers arising from choke-damp and fire-damp, the narrator (the Rev. Dr. Arthur Charlett, Master of University College, Oxford) continues as follows:—

"To prevent both these inconveniences, as the only remedy known here, the viewer of the works takes the best care he can to preserve a free current of air through all the works, and as the air goes down one pit [the 'downcast'] it should ascend another [the 'upcast']. But it happened in this colliery, that there was a pit which stood in an eddy, where the air had not always a free passage, and which in hot and sultry weather was very much subject to sulphur;[1] and it being then the middle of August, and some danger apprehended from the closeness and heat of the season, the men were with the greatest care and caution withdrawn from their work in that pit, and turned into another; but an overman, some days after this change, and upon some notion of his own, being induced, as is supposed, by a fresh, cool, frosty breeze of wind, which blew that unlucky morning, and which always clears the works of all sulphur, had gone too near this pit, and had met the sulphur just as it was purging and dispersing itself, upon which the sulphur immediately took fire by his candle, which proved the destruction of himself and so many men, and caused the greatest fire ever known in these parts."

It was at this colliery that endeavours to produce artificial ventilation by means of fire-lamps, or furnaces, were first made in the North of England, in the year 1732. Soon afterwards these appliances came into use in the collieries on the Tyne. Thus

---

[1] *I.e.* fire-damp.

in a report on Byker Colliery, near Newcastle, dated 1740, the viewers employed set forth that "this colliery will be attended with difficulties occasioned by the great quantity of sulphur; but from experience we find, by using a fire-lamp to rarefy and put the air in motion, hath removed almost all difficulties in that way."

In connection with the above-mentioned explosions we have perhaps the only notices of the employment of females underground in the pits of the Newcastle-on-Tyne district; but in many of the other coal-fields they continued to be employed in the mines long afterwards.

CHAPTER X.

THE COAL TRADE OF THE WEST COAST.—WHITEHAVEN MINES.—CARLISLE AND JAMES SPEDDING.—INVENTION OF THE STEEL MILL, AND COURSING THE AIR.

> " Where late along the naked strand,
> The fisher's cot did lonely stand,
> And his poor bark unshelter'd lay,
> Of every swelling surge the prey,
> Now lofty piers their arms extend,
> And with their strong embraces bend
> Round crowded fleets."
> —DR. DALTON.

WHILE the coal trade had attained to large dimensions on the Tyne and the Frith of Forth, in consequence of the great quantities of coal required for the supply of London and the towns on the coast, as well as for exportation to the Continent, the trade on the west coast was still inconsiderable. As early as the beginning of the seventeenth century a small export trade was being carried on from Swansea and Milford; the port of Chester (which included the collieries on the estuary of the Dee); also from Liverpool and some points of Cumberland; but the quantities shipped were as yet insignificant. The demand for coal for Ireland increased, however, during this century; the supply being chiefly drawn from Mostyn and other collieries on the Dee, and in the latter part of the century also from Whitehaven. At the same time the export of coal had commenced from the port of Irvine, in Ayrshire, but the primitive character of the trade may be inferred from the manner in which it was carried on. A large horn was kept in readiness fixed to a post on the quay by an iron chain, and when coal boats arrived the fact was announced by blowing the horn; upon which signal the country people proceeded to load their coal ponies and carried down to the harbour the quantities of coal required.

In the early part of the eighteenth century the Whitehaven coal trade underwent a great development. This town and harbour owe their existence entirely to the coal trade. In the time of Queen Elizabeth Whitehaven consisted of six fishing cabins, and possessed only one small boat (of nine tons), called the *Bee of Whitehaven*, which carried herrings to Liverpool and Chester and brought back cattle. The working of coal for local requirements, in the land which had previously belonged to the dissolved monastery of St. Bees, was already going on during this reign; but it was not until Whitehaven came into the possession of the Lowther family (early in the seventeenth century) that the systematic development of the mines and the exportation of coal commenced. Up till about 1700 the supply of coal was obtained by means of day-levels, or adits, but at this period a thicker and much superior seam of coal (the Main Seam) was discovered at a depth of about twenty fathoms. To work this new seam pits were sunk at a place subsequently known as "The Gins"; it being so termed from the number of horse-gins employed in freeing the pits from water.

Sir James Lowther, who succeeded his father in 1706, being desirous to improve the working of his collieries, selected as his engineer a promising youth named Carlisle Spedding, fourth son of the principal steward of the Lowther estates. Tradition records that previous to entering on his duties at Whitehaven, Spedding was sent *incognito* to Newcastle-on-Tyne by Sir James, to acquire a knowledge of the methods of mining pursued in that district. Here, under a fictitious name, he obtained employment in the pits as a hewer, or hagger, of coal, making in the meanwhile all the inquiries and discoveries he could relative to the colliery operations. After continuing in this capacity for a considerable time, Spedding, who was then known by the name of "Dan," had the misfortune to be burnt by the fire-damp, whereupon a message was sent to Newcastle to procure the best medical assistance possible in order to recover him. The extraordinary attention paid to a person in the apparent situation of Spedding by such eminent medical practitioners led to the discovery of his true character and motives; accordingly after his recovery, having already accomplished to a large extent the object of his mission, he returned to Whitehaven and set about the improvement of the collieries.

Spedding entered upon the management of the pits at Whitehaven about the year 1718. The building of a steam-engine (or fire-engine as it was then termed) in this year, at a pit in "The Gins," is supposed to have been one of the first acts of his administration. This proved a most decided success, and at once got rid of the expensive and inefficient horse-machines previously employed in draining the mines.

Being endowed with great ingenuity and originality, he soon began to frame comprehensive schemes for carrying on the collieries. At a place called Saltom on the sea shore, half a mile distant from "The Gins," he made a boring, and ascertained the Main Seam of coal to exist there in perfection at a depth of about eighty fathoms. Here he proposed to Sir James Lowther to sink a pit and erect a steam-engine which would drain many hundred acres of coal under the land and an unknown extent under the sea.

The sinking at Saltom was the most remarkable

colliery enterprise of its day. It was commenced in 1729 within twenty yards of high-water mark. The shaft was made oval in form, ten feet by eight feet, in order to admit of pumping and winding being both carried on in it. At a depth of forty-two fathoms the miners pricked a small bed of black stone six inches in thickness, and full of fissures, overlying a seam of coal two feet thick. Contrary to expectation very little water was found at this point, but instead of this a "blower" or strong discharge of fire-damp came off, "which bubbled through a small quantity of water then spread over that part of the pit, and made a great hissing noise." On a candle being held towards it the gas ignited, and burned fiercely on the top of the water. This appears to have been the first encounter with fire-damp at the Whitehaven collieries. The "blower" having been lighted and extinguished several times, and being found to give off an uninterrupted flow of gas, all lights were excluded from the pit till it was sunk quite through the bed of stone and coal, when a tight framing of timber was constructed to dam back the gas out of the pit: a small pipe, two inches square, being led to the surface from behind the framing, which carried off the gas to the open air.

The sinking at Saltom when completed answered to the full the expectations anticipated from it. A number of other pits were sunk in the tract of coal thus drained, by which the output of the colliery was largely increased.

Under Spedding's able management the coal workings at Whitehaven were carried to a much greater depth than had hitherto been attained in any other part of the kingdom, having reached during his term of office a vertical depth of 130 fathoms. The drainage of the mines was effected with little difficulty by means of four Newcomen steam-engines; but the great abundance of fire-damp was a source of much embarrassment, and occasioned many accidents. The accident attended with the greatest loss of life appears to be that which occurred at the Corpsill pit on the 5th of August, 1737, at four o'clock in the morning, when twenty-two people and three horses were killed by a "Great Fire-damp."

No artificial means were employed to produce a ventilating current at Whitehaven, but the mines were unusually favourably situated for obtaining the full advantage of natural ventilation, there being numerous openings to the surface at different altitudes. Notwithstanding this, but for the devices contrived by Spedding for combating the fire-damp, the working of the mines could not have been carried on. The expedient adopted with the blower of gas in the Saltom pit was carried out in other similar cases. Careful search was made for crevices which gave off gas, and such places were dammed off and the discharge of gas carried in pipes to the surface. Such a pipe was conveyed into the laboratory of Dr. Brownrigg, who made many experiments with the gas thus obtained, and also employed it as a substitute for fire in chemical operations. Spedding even proposed to the town authorities to carry pipes to different parts of the town, and light up the streets at night with the natural gas evolved from the mines; but the project does not appear to have gone beyond a proposal, probably owing to the illuminating power of the gas being low, and its discharge somewhat fluctuating.

But Spedding's name is most widely known in connection with the novel method of lighting dangerous parts of mines introduced by him. Observing the low inflammability of fire-damp, which though at once kindled by flame is much less readily ignited in any other way, he invented a small machine called the *steel mill*, in which, on a handle being turned, a thin disc of steel five or six inches in diameter is made to rotate with great velocity; and on a piece of flint being applied to the edge of the revolving disc a continuous flow of brilliant sparks is emitted, sufficient to enable the miners to carry on their work in places where the use of candles could on no account be allowed. As early as 1733 flint and steel were being used at Whitehaven, though it is doubtful whether the steel mill had been invented at this date. In his description of the Whitehaven mines, written

H

twenty years later (about 1753), in which Spedding is referred to under the name of Prospero, Dr. Dalton poetically describes it as—

> "That strange spark-emitting wheel
> Which, formed by Prospero's magic care,
> Plays harmless in the sulphurous air,
> Without a flame diffuses light,
> And makes the grisly cavern bright."

Spedding also appears to have been among the first to employ gunpowder for blasting purposes in coal-mines. It is improbable that this agent was applied at this time in the work of getting the coal; but Dr. Dalton alludes to the "nitrous blast" severing the rock in the cutting of drifts across faults, or dislocations, of the strata.

Spedding introduced at Whitehaven the wooden railways he had seen at Newcastle-on-Tyne; the first being constructed between the Parker pit and the harbour (a distance of half a mile) about 1738.

The coals were drawn from the pits by means of horse-gins, the work being carried on night and day. From the greater depths they were raised in several stages, by underground gins and blind pits, or staples, from one seam to another.

Already in Spedding's time the coal workings had been carried to a considerable distance under the sea. "Sir James's riches," says Sir John Clerk, in a letter dated 1739, "in part swim over his head, for ships pass daily above the very ground where his colliers work."

In the year 1755 Whitehaven lost both Sir James Lowther and Carlisle Spedding. The latter, after conducting the collieries with wonderful ability and energy during the long period of thirty-seven years, had the misfortune to fall a victim to the fire-damp, to disarm which he had laboured so diligently. He was killed by an explosion in the above year, while underground discharging his duties in the mines.

Within a few years after the death of Carlisle Spedding, a great improvement in the method of ventilating coal-mines was introduced by his son, James Spedding, who succeeded to the management of the collieries belonging to the Lowther family on the death of his father. The elder Spedding, in common with his contemporaries, directed the ventilating current specially towards such parts of the mines as were in course of being worked, to the neglect of the portions already excavated and abandoned. This early system of ventilating is termed *face airing*, on account of the air being carried along the front or "face" of the solid coal, where the miners were immediately at work. It was open to the fatal objection that many vacant unventilated spaces were left, in which the noxious gases unobserved and unsuspected might

". . . . train their dread artillery,"

ready, under altered conditions of the atmospheric pressure, to steal out upon the miners' lights and in an instant carry death and destruction through the colliery.

The improved system, first introduced about 1760 in a colliery at Workington (where were situated some recently opened mines belonging to the Lowther family), consisted in forming the whole of the excavated part of the mine into one vast labyrinth, or pipe, by means of doors and stoppings, thus compelling the ventilating current to sweep through every passage of the mine on its way between the downcast and upcast pits. This system is technically termed *coursing the air*.

Possibly James Spedding may have been incited to set about improving the ventilation of collieries from the fact that the steel mill was already ascertained to be not altogether safe to work with. Previous to 1765 it was known at Whitehaven to have been the cause of several explosions; but it continued to be extensively used long afterwards, many being quite unaware of the danger connected with it.

CHAPTER XI.

REVIVAL OF THE IRON TRADE. — GREAT BUILDING OF STEAM-ENGINES IN THE NORTH OF ENGLAND.—INCREASING DEPTH OF THE PITS.—VARIOUS APPLIANCES FOR VENTILATING THE MINES.—EXPLOSIONS OF FREQUENT OCCURRENCE.

In the early half of the eighteenth century the iron trade of Britain was at an extremely low ebb. The charcoal iron manufacture was fast dying out for want of fuel; the manufacture of iron with coke or coal was yet only in its infancy. The total make of pig-iron in England in 1740 is set down at 17,350 tons.

It is generally agreed that the first notable revival of the iron trade took place at Coalbrookdale Foundry, in Shropshire, but a considerable discrepancy prevails as to the precise date when charcoal was superseded by coal fuel in the smelting operations. It appears that the manufacture of iron with coal (or coke) commenced here in the time of the first Abraham

Darby, who settled at Coalbrookdale in 1709 and died in 1717. Charcoal was employed in the blast furnace when Darby first began operations, but soon afterwards coke was used—according to Scrivenor in 1713—the fuel employed in smelting a charge of ore consisting of five baskets of coke, two of brays or small coke, and one of peat. The quantity of iron produced at this period, however, was insignificant, only reaching from five to ten tons per week, and it was not until long subsequently that the production of pit-coal iron at Coalbrookdale assumed any importance. The second period appears to date from 1730-5, about which time a more powerful blast was obtained by the erection of a Newcomen steam-engine to provide an increased supply of water for driving the blast water-wheel.

For a long period Coalbrookdale Foundry continued one of the principal seats of the pit-coal iron industry, but the success achieved here led to the establishment of many new iron-works in different parts of the kingdom for the manufacture of iron by the same process. The greater abundance and cheapness of iron which ensued led to a rapid extension of its use.

Not only were the Coalbrookdale Company the first to manufacture iron with coal on a large scale, but they took the lead in promoting the more general use of cast-iron as a substitute for wood and other materials. It being contrary to the principles of the Darbys, as members of the Society of Friends, to accept contracts, however lucrative, for the manufacture of engines of war, this firm developed the application of iron in the arts of peace. Hence, while the proprietors of the great foundry at Carron became celebrated for their Carronades or "smashers," the Coalbrookdale firm are famous as the constructors of the first iron railways and the builders of the first iron bridge; and their foundry became the great emporium for cast-iron cylinders for steam-engines, cast-iron pipes for mine-pumps, and useful articles of all descriptions made of the same material.

About the year 1740 a commencement had already been made to use cast-iron cylinders in steam-engines (all the earlier cylinders having been made of brass), and there is little doubt that the facility with which large iron cylinders could from this time be obtained helped on to a great extent the marked increase in the building of steam-engines which took place shortly after the middle of the eighteenth century.

Prominent among the builders of engines, as well as in promoting other improvements in the mechanical engineering of collieries in the Newcastle-on-Tyne district at this period, was William Brown, an eminent colliery viewer. Brown was brought up at Throckley, a village situated about six miles west of Newcastle, and was of an aspiring mind and endowed with much natural ability. The means of acquiring a knowledge of the various branches of colliery work were few at this time, but by dint of careful observation and making the most of such opportunities as he had, Brown was already possessed of superior attainments at an early period of his life, and subsequently succeeded in raising himself to the first position among the colliery viewers of his day.

At the outset of his career he had the good fortune to be taken by the hand by Mr. Bell, a gentleman living in the neighbourhood, who leased Throckley Colliery, and appointed him manager, with a handsome salary and one-fourth share of the colliery. On obtaining this position, in 1756, Brown immediately proceeded to erect a steam-engine at the colliery; and no sooner had he shown his engine-building capabilities at Throckley, than his services were in great request for the building of engines to drain other collieries in the district. In the two following years he built six more engines at different collieries; and in the short space of ten years after commencing practice he had fitted up no fewer than twenty-one steam-engines, including three at collieries in Scotland. Subsequently he built several others.

In the meantime other engineers had in like manner been actively engaged in erecting engines at collieries in the Newcastle-on-Tyne district; so much so, that from a list of these machines preserved in

Mr. Brown's books, dated 1769, we find that nearly one hundred had then been built at the northern collieries.

The most remarkable engine and pumping establishment of this period was at the new colliery of Walker-on-Tyne, recently sunk to the Main Coal seam at a depth of one hundred fathoms — the greatest depth yet reached in the Newcastle district. Considering the date of its erection (1763), the engine at Walker was of colossal proportions, its cylinder (brought from Coalbrookdale Foundry) being seventy-four inches in diameter and ten and a-half feet in length. To supply it with steam four large boilers were provided, three of which were always in use. All the pipes in the shaft were made of cast-iron. This engine was pronounced "the most complete and noble piece of iron-work that had up to this time been produced."

The increasing depth of the pits in the North of England necessitated a number of alterations in the methods of conducting the colliery operations. The sinkings, or "winnings," being more tedious and costly, fewer shafts were employed and a larger area was worked by each establishment. The shafts themselves also were made larger, to admit of both pumping and winding being carried on, as well as to allow of the employment of larger coal-baskets.

Sometimes, but rarely, they were made oval in form; usually they were circular, and of a diameter of ten or twelve feet.

To compensate for the greater distances over which coal had to be conveyed underground, wooden railways, resembling those on the surface, were introduced into the mines; and horses were applied on the main underground roads to haul four-wheeled trams carrying one or two baskets of coal.

As the shafts became fewer and deeper, the difficulties arising from the abundance of fire-damp became more and more formidable, and various measures were resorted to, to promote the safety of the collieries. Stoppings of a more substantial character, built of brick and lime, were employed to guide the ventilating current; being first used at Fatfield Colliery, on the Wear, in 1754. At the same colliery, in 1763, after an explosion by which seventeen persons were killed, steel mills brought from Whitehaven were used for the first time in the Newcastle district; and the system of ventilating by "coursing the air" was introduced here about the same time.

Various methods were now in use for producing artificial ventilation: the ordinary arrangement consisting in the employment of a fire-lamp or small furnace to rarefy the air in the upcast shaft. Sometimes, however, the furnace was placed on the surface, at the bottom of a tall chimney communicating with the upcast; an arrangement applied in the North of England for the first time in 1756, at North Biddick Colliery.

At Walker Colliery a different system was pursued, two rotating mechanical ventilators, worked by the steam-engine by means of a train of wheel-work, being employed to produce an air-current as early as 1769. This was the first colliery on the Tyne in which the system of coursing the air was adopted.

Notwithstanding the endeavours which were being made to place the collieries on a safer footing, by employing artificial means to produce a steady air-current to dilute and sweep away the fire-damp, by building more substantial stoppings and coursing the air through all the workings, and by substituting steel mills for candles, explosions took place in one colliery after another, sometimes two or three occurring in a single year. The best means known being ineffectual to prevent these calamities, allusions to them by the public press were regarded with displeasure. Commenting on this matter, the *Newcastle Journal*, under date 21st March, 1767, makes the following observations:—

"As so many deplorable accidents have lately happened in collieries, it certainly claims the attention of coalowners to make provision for the distressed widows and fatherless children occasioned by these mines, as the catastrophes from foul air become more common than ever. Yet, as we have been requested to take no particular notice of these things, which, in fact, could have very little good tendency, we drop the further mentioning of it."

So far from being able to cope with the fierce and invisible enemy with which they were brought face to face, the viewers themselves at times fell victims to the fiery blasts which devastated the mines.

CHAPTER XII.

FIRST EMPLOYMENT OF IRON IN RAILWAY CONSTRUCTION.—THE STEAM-ENGINE INDIRECTLY APPLIED TO DRAW THE COALS OUT OF THE PITS THROUGH THE MEDIUM OF WATER-WHEELS.—CURR'S IMPROVEMENTS IN SHAFT FITTINGS AND UNDERGROUND CONVEYANCE.

RAILWAYS were now in use in many of the coal-fields, but this system of conveyance had received its greatest development in the Newcastle-on-Tyne district, where all the collieries were connected by rail with their shipping places on the Tyne or Wear. An inadequate idea of the character of the railways of this period has been entertained by many writers who have referred to them. This appears to have originated in the remarks of Arthur Young, who, in the account of his northern tour in 1768, states that "the coal-waggon roads, from the pits to the water, are great works, carried over all sorts of inequalities of ground." From this casual description it seems to have been inferred that the railways followed the undulations of the ground. Such, however, was by no means the case.

A very exact account of the manner of constructing railways in the North of England, in 1765, is given by an intelligent French traveller, M. Jars, who terms them *nouvelles routes*. In order to facilitate the conveyance of the loaded waggons, the railways were laid off as much as possible with a uniform descent towards the depôts at the river; great expense being incurred to accomplish this desirable arrangement. Oak sleepers, from four to eight inches square, were placed at distances of two or three feet from each other, and to these the rails, six or seven inches broad by four or five inches thick, and sawn truly square, were secured by means of wooden pins. The ordinary gauge of the rails was about four feet. Some of the railways were nine or ten miles in length, and served to convey the coal from several collieries. These early railways were of the "edge rail," or modern type, the flanges being upon the wheels of the waggons.

Up till the year 1767 all the railways in the kingdom were constructed wholly of wood, with the exception of the employment of small bands of iron to strengthen the joints of the rails. But wooden rails were liable to rapid deterioration, and the demand for iron at Coalbrookdale happening to be slack in this year, it occurred to Richard Reynolds, one of the partners, that rails of cast-iron might be employed with advantage. A small quantity were accordingly cast as an experiment. They were four inches in breadth, an inch and a-quarter in thickness, and four feet in length, and were laid upon and secured to the previously existing wooden rails. They were found to improve the railway so much that the same course was pursued with all the railways at the works. Between this period and the end of the eighteenth century considerable progress was made in the substitution of iron for wood in railway construction.

While the application of the Newcomen steam-engine to work the pumps had afforded a satisfactory solution of the problem of raising water from the collieries, no adequate machinery had yet been invented for drawing the coal out of the deeper pits now being sunk. At Walker Colliery, alike the deepest and most important in the North of England at this time, a machine worked by eight horses was employed in the work. The horses were kept at a sharp trot, and a large horizontal wheel was used to give greater velocity to the drum or rope-roll; but all the machine could do was to bring up a load of 6 cwts. of coal from a depth of 100 fathoms in two minutes.

An attempt made at Hartley Colliery to apply the steam-engine to this work attracted considerable attention at the time. The arrangement was patented by a Mr. Joseph Oxley, in 1763, and the first machine was built at Hartley in the same year. A second and improved one was fitted up at the same place in 1765, which raised coal at the rate of a basket a minute, and was for a short time regarded as the greatest improvement in the coal trade since the invention of the steam-engine. The machine, however, was subject to frequent breakages. The celebrated James Watt, who went to see it in 1768, speaks of it as performing its work sluggishly and irregularly, having no fly-wheel.

The steam-engine being at this period only a *single-acting* machine, was ill-adapted for producing an even rotative motion directly. The attempts to use its power indirectly in raising coal were more successful. One of the earliest arrangements to effect this—the invention of Mr. Michael Menzies—was applied at Chatershaugh Colliery, on the Wear, in 1753. The basket of coals was raised by the descent of a bucket of water, a steam-engine being employed to re-pump the water to the surface. By this means a basket containing $5\frac{1}{2}$ cwts. of coal was drawn from a depth of fifty fathoms in two minutes. An arrangement on the same principle, known as the *balance-tub system*, was subsequently largely employed, more especially in collieries where the water used in raising the coals could be run off by an adit without requiring to be pumped up again.

The most approved method, however, and the one which came into most general use at the deeper collieries, consisted in applying the steam-engine to raise water into elevated cisterns for driving waterwheels, by means of which the coals were drawn. Double water-wheels, with their buckets arranged in reverse order, had been in use at the Alloa Collieries, on the Frith of Forth, since the beginning of the century. The introduction of these machines, as well as the construction of large reservoirs to provide a supply of water for the engines at this colliery establishment, was probably due to Sorocould, as they appear to date from the time of his visit to Alloa. It is stated that Mr. Brown, of Throckley, when at Alloa, in 1774, was so much struck with the double water-wheel that he made a drawing of it, and on his return home designed one on the same principle to suit the deep pits at Newcastle. But the idea of employing water-wheels for drawing coal had already begun to receive attention, and in this same year we find Smeaton erecting one at Sir Roger Newdigate's Colliery, at Griff, in Warwickshire, for this purpose. To economise water, Smeaton employed a single water-wheel which always travelled in the same direction, the reversing of the drum being effected by means of gearing; but, owing to its greater simplicity, the double-bucket wheel was almost universally adopted.

In the above cases natural supplies of water were available, but so simple, so powerful, and so easily managed was the water-wheel that it soon became apparent that it afforded the best medium for drawing coals yet invented, even in situations where steam-engines might be required to provide a supply of water. Among Smeaton's Reports is a "Comparative estimate of drawing coals by horses, or by a coal-engine worked by water supplied by a fire-engine." It is dated 14th August, 1776, and shows a considerable saving by the latter method. In the following year Smeaton designed a "water coal gin" of the above description for the Prosperous Pit, at Long Benton Colliery, near Newcastle. It was found to be a great improvement on the horse-gin previously in use, doing the work of sixteen horses and four men, and drawing a basket carrying $6\frac{1}{2}$ cwt. of coal from a depth of 82 fathoms in two minutes. Mr. Brown had been engaged at the same time in the construction of a similar machine for the colliery recently opened out by him and the Bell family at Willington. It was started in November, 1778, and "exceeded the most sanguine expectations," uniformly drawing thirty 6-cwt. baskets an hour from a depth of 101 fathoms.

These machines came rapidly into use at all the deeper collieries in the North of England, and to a smaller extent in other parts of the kingdom. For a period of nearly twenty years they were the most efficient means known for drawing coal from great depths. But on the expiration of the patent for the application of the crank to the steam-engine, in the year 1794, the facility with which Watt's *double-acting* steam-engine could be applied directly to the drum shaft caused it rapidly to supersede all other methods. The use of water-wheels went out as quickly as it came in, and the drawing of the coal out of the pits was added to the duties already performed by the steam-engine.

Reference has been made to the introduction of wooden railways underground in the North of England collieries to expedite the conveyance of coal between the *faces*, or hewers' working places, and the shaft bottom, and to the employment of horses on the main roads. The barrowmen, or putters, brought single baskets from the face to the horse station, where by means of a crane they were lifted upon a large tram, or rolley, carrying two or three baskets, on which they were conveyed to the pit bottom. Here they were hooked on to the rope by the corf-bow and swung up the shaft to the surface. The damage occasioned by the baskets striking against each other, or against the sides of the pit, during their passage up and down, had been a source of inconvenience from a very early period, but had not been so much felt while the winding was carried on by horse-gins at a slow rate. To lessen the force of collision between the ascending and descending baskets in passing, Smeaton introduced a self-acting arrangement in his water-gins whereby the speed was momentarily reduced at this point.

While the above system was being pursued in the collieries of the North of England, an entirely different and in some respects superior arrangement had been invented and applied by Mr. John Curr at the Duke of Norfolk's collieries at Sheffield. Mr. Curr belonged to the North of England, having been brought up at Pontop Pike, near Tanfield, in Durham. He went to the Duke of Norfolk's collieries in a subordinate capacity, but was subsequently intrusted with their entire management, when he introduced a series of improvements in the mechanical arrangements which exhibited a remarkable degree of ingenuity and originality.

The most notable of these consisted in the substitution of cast-iron rails for wooden ones, both underground and on the surface (introduced by him in 1776); the employment of small carriages with four wheels in which the coals were conveyed direct from the faces to the pit bottom; the application of guides, or conductors, in the shaft, which enabled the carriages to be raised to the surface at a high speed without any danger of collision; and the use of flat ropes instead of round ones to ease the load upon the winding engine.

Mr. Curr's rails were of the *plate rail* or *tram plate* form, and were six feet long, three inches broad on the trod, and half an inch thick. The margin or flange was two inches higher than the plate.

The carriages held five and a half or six hundredweight of coal, and were provided with wheels from ten to thirteen inches in diameter. The flange being transferred to the rails, the carriage wheels were made plain and with a narrow periphery to lessen friction. Coupling-chains were provided for attaching the carriages together, thus enabling a horse to haul a train of ten or twelve at a time.

The conductors, or guides, consisted of two or three continuous wooden rails, or rods, four inches by three, secured on opposite sides of the pit. At the rope ends cross-bars were provided, fitted with rollers at their extremities which ran upon the conductors, and below these the carriages were suspended. On arriving at the surface the carriage was raised a little distance above the mouth of the pit, when a wooden platform or trap-door was introduced beneath it, on to which its wheels were lowered. It was then detached from the rope and run off, and an empty carriage having been substituted for it and raised so as to admit of the platform being withdrawn, the winding recommenced; the speed of winding being as much as seventy fathoms in half a minute.

As the depth of the mines increased, the weight of the ropes employed in raising the coals became of itself a considerable load upon the winding machine. In addition to the weight of coals, the engine had to raise the weight of the whole length of rope hanging in the pit at the commencement of its run, the other rope at this point being wound upon the drum and rendering no assistance. Several expedients to counteract this were brought forward in the latter part of the eighteenth century. Smeaton applied conical drums; others used counterbalance weights of various kinds. With the same object Mr. Curr invented the flat rope. It consisted of several small round ropes stitched together, and was made to lap upon itself in winding. Thus at the commencement of a run the loaded rope began to coil upon a small diameter gradually increasing, while the empty rope began to coil off a large diameter gradually decreasing—an arrangement which rendered great assistance to the winding engine.

A number of other improvements were introduced

by Mr. Curr at the collieries under his care. Among these was the use of self-acting incline planes, whereby a train of full carriages in descending was made to pull up an empty train at the same time, the two being connected by means of a rope passing round a sheave, or pulley-wheel, at the top. By the employment of cast-iron rails these incline planes could be employed whenever the fall of the road amounted to three inches per yard.

Mr. Curr's improvements were a great step in the direction of modern arrangements. His rails and flat ropes soon came into general use throughout the kingdom; but his shaft fittings were not sufficiently matured to admit of their introduction into the deeper mines, though they answered the purpose remarkably well in the shallow collieries about Sheffield, and other parts in the south.

The introduction of Mr. Curr's cast-iron rails (or *plates* as they were termed) underground relieved enormously the slavish labour of the barrow-men, or coal-putters, who conveyed the coal between the working places and the horse roads. It would appear from the following stanzas that the improvement was received with much gratitude:—

> "But heavy puttin' 's now forgotten
> Sic as we had i' former days;
> Ower holey thill an' dylls a-splittin',
> Trams now a-run on metal ways.

"God bless the man in peace and plenty
 That first invented metal plates;
 Draw out his years to five times twenty,
 Then slide him through the heavenly gates.

"For if the human frame to spare
 Frae toil an' pain ayont conceivin',
 Hae aught to dae wi' gettin' there,
 I'm sure he maun gan' strite to heaven."

CHAPTER XIII.

GREAT DIFFICULTIES ENCOUNTERED IN OPENING OUT THE FAMOUS WALLSEND COLLIERY.—JOHN BUDDLE, SENR.—CAST-IRON TUBBING.

IN the district situated between the town of Newcastle and the mouth of the River Tyne, there lay a tract of land beneath which existed an important seam of coal known as the "Main Coal," the peculiar excellence of which for household purposes rendered it the most valuable seam in the Great Northern Coal-field at this epoch. The tract in question—locally termed "the Tyne basin"—being intersected by the River Tyne, presented unusual facilities for the shipment of coals; but the depth of the seam from the surface had hitherto operated to retard its development.

Near the centre of this tract stood the village of Wallsend (so named from its position at the eastern end of the Roman Wall), in the vicinity of which the opening out of the famous Wallsend Colliery was commenced in the latter part of the eighteenth century.

Though this colliery eventually became exceedingly prosperous and profitable, and the excellent quality of its coal led to the name "Wallsend" being adopted as a password by other collieries, the winning of the pits proved one of the most arduous mining enterprises which had up to this time been attempted. Difficulties arising from quicksands, water, and inflammable gas, taxed to the utmost the arts of the miners, and occasioned numerous disasters during the infancy of the colliery.

Sinking operations were commenced at Wallsend in 1778, but the first pit was lost in a quicksand. A second attempt narrowly escaped the same fate; but by means of successive tiers of piles the shaft was carried through the sand, though its diameter was reduced in the process to five feet eleven inches. Two shafts—the A pit and the B pit, the latter being nine feet in diameter—were at length carried down to the seam at a depth of about one hundred fathoms, and the working of coal began in 1781.

Pumping engines were applied in both pits, but they were of inadequate power; a circumstance which, aggravated as it was by great abundance of fire-damp met with, caused the greatest difficulty to be experienced in carrying on the colliery. In October, 1783, a "blower" of fire-damp ignited at the candle of a hewer, who fled precipitately without attempting to extinguish the flaming gas. The overman made a courageous attempt to reach the seat of the fire, but was overpowered by the smoke and noxious gases and suffocated; and it having become evident that the coal itself had been set on fire, the burning district was flooded with water in order to extinguish it.

The above accident did not long delay the colliery operations, but two years later an explosion occurred which entailed a long series of disasters. On the 9th of October, 1785, the discharge of fire-damp so overloaded the ventilating current as to raise it to the firing point, when it ignited at the ventilating furnace and produced a severe "blast" in the *upcast*, or B pit. Fortunately the few men who were in the mine at the time were occupied at the bottom of the other pit, and succeeded in escaping to the surface without serious injury; but the woodwork supporting the pumps in the B pit was blown out, and the coal at the pit bottom set on fire, so that it became necessary to seal up the mouths of the pits, and to flood the workings with water a second time in order to extinguish it.

The pits remained covered up till the 2nd of November, when three men descended the B pit to examine the state of the shaft by the light of a steel mill; but no sooner had they reached a depth of seventy fathoms from the surface than an explosion took place which killed the whole of the exploring party. Up till this time implicit reliance had been placed in the safety of the steel mill by the Wallsend miners, in consequence of which this explosion caused great consternation. The use of the instrument, however, was continued, and the repairs in the shaft were proceeded with by its light.

On the 11th of November, while the engine-wright and an assistant were engaged in changing a bucket in the A pit by the light of a steel mill, another explosion occurred which killed both, and occasioned a great panic. Still the mill was scarcely suspected, the pitmen preferring to imagine that the explosion originated from fire in the workings under water, or some other mysterious cause. Its use was accordingly continued in executing the repairs in the B pit till the 21st of December, when another explosion occurred, by which the overman and a sinker who were at work in the shaft were both killed.

This accident shook the confidence of the miners in the mill to such a degree that for some time they dared not venture to employ it, preferring to work by such other feeble light as they could obtain. The daylight received from above being dim and imperfect, fish in a phosphorescent state and various preparations of phosphorus were tried, but with little benefit. Another method, accidentally discovered, afforded material service. It happened that a carpenter engaged upon some work at the top of the pit in which he made use of a bright new hand-saw, turned the blade to such an angle as to throw a flash of light down the pit. The sudden gleam so alarmed the men below, who thought the pit had fired, that they demanded to be drawn to the top with all speed. The discovery of the cause of the alarm led to the employment of a mirror at the top of the pit, which proved of great service during periods of sunshine.

The progress of restoring the colliery, however, being slow and tedious, the season being the depth of winter, the steel mill began again to be partially used; but on the 14th of February, 1786, another explosion took place in the B pit by which three men were severely burnt. The mill was in consequence once more thrown into discredit, and the work proceeded very much in the dark. None but the most intrepid colliers would venture down the pit. Two men descended at a time in a sinking corve, with a rope round their bodies to attach them to the chain. They grubbed about and filled the corve with their hands as well as they could, and then returned to the top with it. This trip constituted their *shift*, for which they were paid 5*s*. each with a *pour boire* into the bargain.

By continuous struggles in this manner the pits were at length cleared, and the water lowered sufficiently to allow a current of air to pass between the pits, after which the operations for restoring the colliery to working order went forward more briskly. The steel mill was again introduced as the only light available underground, and all went well till the 9th of June,

1786, when an explosion took place in the workings near the bottom of the A pit. This explosion did not kill any of the workmen who were in the pit at the time, and was distinctly ascertained to have been occasioned by a spark from a steel mill. The overman was "playing" the mill at the moment, and saw the gas igniting at the sparks which it produced. The explosion did little damage beyond paralysing the exertions of the workmen for a time. Work, however, was soon resumed, and on the 19th of July, 1786, the drawing of coal was again commenced at the A pit after a cessation of upwards of nine months.

In the meantime the repairs in the B pit were continued till the 3rd of November, when another explosion occurred by which six lives were lost. The men were engaged in making a communication between the two pits, and were under the necessity of working among inflammable gas. Having no alternative but to use the steel mill or to work in absolute darkness they preferred the former course, but the result proved fatal to them. The excavation was subsequently effected without light of any kind, and bore the name of the "Dark Wall" ever after. The repairs to the B pit were completed, and work again resumed on the 7th of January, 1787, the ventilation being improved by placing a powerful furnace at the shaft bottom and other measures.

The foregoing and one or two accidents which

subsequently occurred pointed to the necessity of having additional shafts, the sinking of which was accordingly proceeded with; and after the C and D pits came into operation, in 1790, the colliery was carried on with great success, and no more fatal accidents occurred for a considerable number of years.

Shortly after this period (about the year 1792) John Buddle, senr., father of the celebrated John Buddle, entered upon the management of Wallsend Colliery, which soon became the most important colliery on the River Tyne. Comparatively little appears to be known regarding the elder Buddle. He is stated to have been a person of great intelligence, and possessed of considerable literary and scientific attainments. He took delight in solving mathematical and scientific problems, and kept up a correspondence with Hutton, Emerson, and others, on subjects in which they took a common interest. He was a frequent contributor to the *Ladies'* and *Gentlemen's Diaries*, and from a mathematical question propounded by him in the latter periodical we learn that he was born in the year 1743. In early life he resided at Chester-le-Street, the centre of the mining district of the River Wear, where for some time he held the position of schoolmaster. From thence he removed to Kyo, a small village near Tanfield, and here his son John was born in 1773. We are unable to state the precise date at which the elder Buddle abandoned the "delightful task," for the more arduous but more remunerative profession of colliery viewer, but it must have occurred several years subsequent to the birth of his son, inasmuch as the only regular schooling young Buddle got, is said to have consisted in one year's attendance at his father's school when very young. At this period Mr. Buddle published an edition of the Marquis of Worcester's *Century of Inventions*, to which he appended some historical notes relative to the invention of the steam-engine. The preface to the work (which was subsequently republished by his son) is dated " Kyo, near Lanchester, 1778."

From Kyo, Mr. Buddle removed to Greenside, near Ryton, to superintend the colliery operations there. In explanation of his acquaintance with the theory and practice of coal-mining it has been stated that he had originally been a pitman; but however this may be, the skill with which he discharged the duties of colliery viewer is sufficiently attested by the fact of his being selected by Mr. Russell to fill the difficult position of manager at his colliery at Wallsend, whither he removed about the year 1792, as already stated, and where young Buddle, now a lad of nineteen, acted in the capacity of assistant to his father.

The successful establishment of Wallsend Colliery was followed by the opening out of a number of other deep collieries in the immediate neighbourhood, on both sides of the River Tyne, to work the same valuable seam of coal. Of these Hebburn Colliery, 129 fathoms in depth, was won in 1792-4; Percy Main Colliery, 120 fathoms, in 1796-9; Jarrow Colliery, 128 fathoms, in 1803; and South Shields Colliery, 140 fathoms, in 1810.

The opening out of the above important collieries caused the Tyne basin to become the great theatre of mining operations in the north at this epoch. The sinking of the pits was in most cases attended with much difficulty, on account of the watery strata passed through, from which large feeders of water were discharged into the shafts, necessitating the employment of tubbing to dam it out. In the case of Hebburn Colliery these feeders amounted to 3,000 gallons per minute. Up till this time the universal practice had been to construct the tubbing with timber, and the same custom was pursued in the case of the shafts at Hebburn, Jarrow, and South Shields; the timber being applied either in the form of plank tubbing or of solid cribbing. Cast iron, however, which was gradually supplanting wood on the surface and underground railways, and was likewise now beginning to be used in the construction of bridges, offered a superior material for damming out the water in the shafts, and a commencement was accordingly made to substitute this for wood tubbing. In the year 1792 a cast-iron tub, consisting of cylinders the full size of the pit, was applied by the elder Buddle to dam back a quicksand in the A pit at Wallsend. Similar cylinders were employed by Mr. Barnes in the

King pit at Walker Colliery about 1795. This form of tubbing, however, was only available near the surface, but by dividing the rings into segments it became applicable in any part of the shaft. Segments of cast iron, having flanges turned inwards for bolting the pieces together, were first used by Mr. Buddle, in 1796-7, in sinking the Percy Main pit. An improved form of segments, having the flanges turned outwards and without bolts, was introduced by the same gentleman in sinking the Howdon pit in 1804-5 ; an arrangement which has ever since been universally adopted where cast-iron tubbing is applied under ordinary circumstances.

CHAPTER XIV.

VARIOUS METHODS OF DEALING WITH INFLAMMABLE GAS.—THE DILUTING SYSTEM, THE NEUTRALIZING SYSTEM, THE FIRING SYSTEM, THE DRAINING SYSTEM.

DURING the years 1805-6 a number of disastrous colliery explosions occurred in close succession in various parts of the kingdom. In the North of England, Hebburn Colliery exploded on the 21st of October, 1805, occasioning a loss of thirty-five lives; Oxclose Colliery on the 28th of November following, with the loss of thirty-eight lives; and Killingworth Colliery on the 28th of March, 1806, with the loss of ten lives. Other explosions occurred in 1806, viz., two at Mostyn, in North Wales, by which thirty-six men perished; another at St. Helens, in Lancashire, with the loss of sixteen lives; and another at Whitehaven, with the loss of eleven lives. The frequent repetition of these calamities led to the proposal of several new schemes for dealing with the noxious gases, and particularly with the fire-damp, of coal mines.

Two methods of combating the inflammable gas have already been referred to, and were now in use in different parts of the kingdom. The first of these, consisting in the introduction of a ventilating current sufficiently ample to reduce the gas below the point of ignition and sweep it out of the mine as quickly as it was produced, has been termed the *diluting system*. The second method, practised where the ventilation alone was inadequate to remove the gas, consisted in kindling and exploding it at intervals sufficiently short to prevent large accumulations from being formed, and was known as the *firing system*.

Near the close of the year 1805 a new scheme was brought under the notice of the owners and agents of the collieries in the North of England by Dr. Trotter, a physician resident in Newcastle-on-Tyne. The attention of this gentleman was drawn to the subject, he tells us, in connection with the explosion at Hebburn Colliery. When on a visit to a sick friend he happened to pass the churchyard at Jarrow, at the time that thirty-two pitmen, victims of this explosion, were being interred there. The solemnity of the scene, and the fact that the unfortunate men had left twenty-five widows and eighty-one orphans to bewail their loss, so impressed him as to induce him to prepare and issue a pamphlet addressed to the coal-owners and agents, entitled *A Proposal for Destroying the Fire and Choak Damps of Coal Mines*.

In this pamphlet Dr. Trotter suggested a scheme for depriving fire-damp of its explosive properties by a process of fumigation, to be performed by means of oxygenated muriatic gas—a *neutralizing system* it may be termed. But though the proposal does credit to his humanity, and proved of service in leading to a discussion of the subject, the scheme was open to a number of fatal objections. These were urged with much force by two writers who undertook to reply to Dr. Trotter's proposal, viz., Dr. Dewar, physician to the Manchester Infirmary, and an anonymous writer who styles himself "A Friend to Rational Schemes of Improvement," both of whom display a knowledge of chemistry, and of the interior economy of coal mines, superior to that possessed by Dr. Trotter. The chief objections urged against the proposed scheme were, that the gases resulting from the fumigation would be extremely deleterious, and that the cost of the process, assuming the possibility of carrying it out in practice, would be so enormous as to put its employment altogether out of the question.

Dr. Trotter's able critics offered some valuable suggestions of their own for the consideration of the owners and agents of coal mines. Dr. Dewar proposed the employment of steam, instead of fire, for rarefying the air at the mouth of the upcast shaft in the case of the ventilation of old workings, where explosion might be apprehended at a ventilating furnace. "Let the air from the shaft," he says, "pass through a tall cylinder of tinned iron. Let this be contained within another cylinder sufficiently large to leave a considerable vacant space between the two, and let this space be accurately closed in all directions, with only two openings, one for admitting the steam from a boiler, and the other for allowing the condensed water to escape. It is hardly necessary to observe that the external cylinder must be surrounded with baked clay, brick, or some other slow-conducting substance, to prevent a superfluous expenditure of heat. This mode of ventilation would be slower than that in common use, but it would evidently be much more safe in the cases here referred to. Would it not be equally certain in its effect? and (where the price of fuel is no object) would it not be sufficiently economical?"

A suggestion of still greater value emanated from Dr. Trotter's second critic, "A Friend to Rational Schemes of Improvement." This writer proposed an improved arrangement of the underground ventilation, so as to dispense with the numerous doors required to guide the air current. The inconvenience arising from the use of doors, he states, "might probably be obviated by dividing the mine into a greater number of *independent systems of ventilation*, so disposed that each waggon-road shall form part of an air-course, and shall not intersect any air-course. This measure must of course be attended with some expense in making partitions, &c.; but this would be of no great amount, and would be cheaply purchased, when it is considered that it would insure the lives of numbers of persons who may now be brought into danger by the trifling circumstance of inadvertently leaving open a door."

Shortly after the date when the above pregnant suggestion was published (1806), the plan of adopting "independent systems of ventilation" was actually carried out in practice, and was found to be productive of immense benefit in many ways; indeed, it has been aptly termed the true secret of mine ventilation. The introduction of this improvement, however, will be referred to hereafter.

Contemporaneously with Dr. Trotter's proposal to employ chemical agents to destroy the noxious gases, a new scheme for dealing with the inflammable gas was devised by a Mr. James Ryan. We are unable to state how Ryan was employed in his earlier years, but in 1800 he was engaged as a mineral surveyor under the Grand Canal Company in Ireland. In 1804 we find him employed to examine and report upon Mostyn and some other collieries in North Wales; and in the following year he invented and patented an improved method of boring, whereby *cores* could be obtained, and the quality of the strata pierced be ascertained with more certainty than formerly. He also proposed to employ his apparatus for boring out shafts several feet in diameter, which might be used for pumping or ventilating mines.

Having in the course of his professional duties acquired a knowledge of the properties of the gases met with in coal mines, Ryan projected a new scheme for clearing the mines of fire-damp. This gas, on account of its light specific gravity, tending always to flow upwards and collect in the higher parts of the workings, he proposed to employ a series of small passages, or gas drifts, so arranged as to collect and draw off the gas at the highest level. His system may be termed the *draining system*.

For some time Ryan was unable to obtain an opportunity of putting his scheme into practice. In 1806 he visited the scenes of the various explosions in the west, at Mostyn, St. Helens, and Whitehaven, but his proposals were rejected. In the same year he also visited Newcastle-on-Tyne, and had many conversations with Mr. Buddle on the subject of mine ventilation, in consequence of which he delivered a course of lectures at Newcastle; but he failed to induce any colliery to adopt his system, and was forced to return home without having obtained a trial of his scheme in any pit. In the following year (1807) he proceeded to London and waited upon Sir John Sinclair, the liberal-minded President of the Board of Agriculture, who highly approved of his plans, and introduced him to the Honourable Washington Shirley, through whose influence he at last succeeded in obtaining an opportunity of applying his system in some of the mines in South Staffordshire.

Ryan's system of ventilation was peculiarly suited to the South Staffordshire mines. The method of working pursued in this county was of a unique type, having its origin in the exceptional conditions under which the coal existed and the character of the coal itself. The seam of coal most extensively worked, viz., the Thick Coal, was of extraordinary thickness, as much as thirty or forty feet; while the small coal, or slack, which was produced in working and was invariably left underground, was remarkably subject to spontaneous combustion, or "breeding fire," as it was termed by the miners. The coal being comparatively shallow, and a large quantity obtainable from a small area, the workings were never carried to any great distance from the shafts; and the arrangement of the workings was specially designed to check the spread of the underground fires which were of such frequent occurrence. This was effected by dividing the area to be worked into a number of large chambers surrounded on all sides by *fire ribs*, or barriers of solid coal, through which no openings were made save only such as were essentially necessary for the extraction of the coal and the passage of air, and these were effectually stopped up and the whole chamber dammed off as soon as all the coal that could be got from it had been obtained.

To reduce still further the risk of premature ignition of the slack, the working of the coal was carried on with a minimum of ventilation; and inasmuch as the air current from the downcast pit was brought by means of a passage termed the "air-head" into the upper part of the chamber, and the quantity of air introduced was insufficient to dilute and sweep away the fire-damp, recourse was regularly had to the firing process to dissipate the collections of inflammable gas in the upper parts of the chambers.

The firing process as practised in Staffordshire, being essential to the method of working and ventilating pursued, was conducted upon a regular system. During the operation of exploding the gas, all the workmen, save those actually engaged—the *firemen* as they were termed—were withdrawn from the mine. The pit stables were employed by the firemen as their base of operations, and were strongly barricaded for the purpose. From this point a copper wire—the *firing line*—was led to the part of the mine where the accumulation of gas existed. Approaching as near to the place of danger as was consistent with their own safety, the firemen raised the wire aloft by means of a long pole (or series of poles fitting each other like a fishing-rod), and provided with a small sheave or wheel at the extremity for carrying the line. Having fixed the pole in the required position, and secured to the end of the line on the floor of the mine a lighted candle weighted with a piece of lead to keep it steady, the firemen retired to the stable, where, pulling in the wire through a crevice, they elevated the lighted candle at the other end and so exploded the gas. If by any accidental circumstance the candle had become extinguished, and the explosion did not take place, the firemen were sometimes left in a state of the greatest suspense, and being afraid to sally out, remained pent up for a length of time imprisoned in their own stronghold.

In many instances the above dangerous operation had to be repeated several times in a day. Thus at the Netherton pits belonging to Lord Dudley, between the years 1798 and 1808, the firing of the gas was regularly practised three times a day, viz. at four o'clock in the morning, at noon, and at seven in the evening.

Such was the condition of mine ventilation in South Staffordshire when Ryan came into the district at the close of the year 1808. Having been intrusted with the management of one of the most fiery mines, he proceeded to put his ideas to a practical test, and by a few alterations which he made, succeeded in clearing the mine from fire-damp, and putting the workings into a safe state, in the short space of twenty days. This he effected chiefly by a rearrangement of the ventilating current, connecting the air-heads, or passages in the higher parts of the coal, with the upcast instead of the downcast pit, and thus employing them to draw off the gas, instead of blowing in air among it as formerly. In this way the light specific gravity of the fire-damp, which had previously been a source of difficulty, was made to aid in the escape of the gas.

That the introduction of Ryan's system was productive of great benefit to the South Staffordshire mines cannot be disputed. It threw a new light on the subject of ventilation, and led to the general adoption of *top-heads*, or passages in the upper portion of the Thick Coal for draining off the gas. This alteration rendered the use of the firing-line unnecessary, inasmuch as accumulations of gas could no longer take place. Like other innovators and improvers, however, Ryan was not without detractors and rivals.

But though the draining system proved of great service under the peculiar circumstances attending the working of the Staffordshire Thick Coal, it was less applicable in the case of thin coal lying in a level or undulating position, where the workings were carried over extensive areas, and fire-damp was met with in great quantities, and where no natural difficulty prevented the introduction of large volumes of air into the mines. Hence it is not surprising to find that while Ryan's system was highly esteemed by many intelligent persons in the midland districts, his schemes were regarded with complete apathy by the viewers of the North of England, who universally adhered to the diluting system of ventilation. A few years later (1815) he attempted to introduce his system into the north, but without success. His labours in the cause of the better ventilation of mines were duly appreciated by the London Society of Arts, who, in the year 1816, presented him with their gold medal and one hundred guineas: and the value of his suggestions has been acknowledged by later investigators, both in this country and on the Continent, to a greater extent than was accorded to him by some of his contemporaries in the mining world.

CHAPTER XV.

THE SYSTEM OF COURSING THE AIR BECOMES INADEQUATE.—CREEPS.—MR. BUDDLE INTRODUCES COMPOUND OR DOUBLE VENTILATION, AND PANEL-WORKING.

In the year 1806, on the death of his father, Mr. John Buddle succeeded to the management of Wallsend Colliery, and to an extensive practice as a mining engineer. At this period the collieries in the North of England were conducted in the manner which had been pursued with little alteration for a considerable length of time, but which was gradually becoming inadequate, owing to the increasing depth and extent of the mines, and the large quantities of inflammable gas met with.

The ventilating power universally employed consisted of a large furnace, which was occasionally placed in connection with a chimney at the surface, but more usually at the bottom of the upcast shaft. The use of the furnace was known to be an element of danger in fiery mines, but no other means had been discovered so effectual in producing a powerful ventilating current.

The common arrangement of the ventilation was that invented by Mr. James Spedding, and already referred to as *coursing the air*. Though a great improvement upon the ancient or primitive method in which large portions of the abandoned workings, or *waste*, were left altogether unventilated, this system was being carried beyond the limits within which it could be safely applied; and as the extent of the workings increased, its inadequacy and defects were being more and more felt. To guide the air-current in its long labyrinthine passage through the mine, a vast number of doors and stoppings were required, the failure or neglect of any one of which might be productive of the most disastrous results; and apart from this source of danger the enormous length of the passage which the air had to traverse between its entrance at the downcast and its exit at the upcast shaft, constituted a radical defect in the system. At Walker Colliery, for example, though the shafts were only half a mile apart, the ventilating current travelled a distance of more than thirty miles on its way underground from the one to the other. Conveying the air through long passages of this kind not only heavily taxed the ventilating power on account of the great friction with which it was attended, but in the case of fiery mines gave rise to a more direct and imminent danger. In passing through the mine the ventilating current became more and more loaded with fire-damp on its way, so much so that at times the last of the air was raised almost to the firing point, and flashed into large sheets of fire as it rushed over the furnace. When explosion was threatened from this cause, the only resource known was to throw open the main doors, thus suspending the ventilation and allowing the fresh air to pass directly from the downcast to the upcast pit, until the furnace could be extinguished; when the doors were again closed, and other temporary expedients applied, such as a waterfall in the downcast pit, by means of which the vitiated air was driven safely over the cold furnace. To relight the furnace in such a case was a task of much anxiety and danger. This was sometimes accomplished by charging it with tar and various highly inflammable materials, which were ignited by means of a red-hot iron ring run down a line from the surface. Mr. Buddle relates how on one particular occasion he watched the furnace at Hebburn Colliery almost daily for about six weeks before he got it lighted, and only accomplished it at last by taking advantage of a favourable state of the atmosphere.

The difficulties in the way of carrying on the colliery operations with safety were greatly increased by movements of the workings termed *creeps*, which were of common occurrence at this time in the deeper collieries of the north. Creeps took place when the pillars of coal left were insufficient to support the weight of the superincumbent strata. Under these circumstances the pillars gradually sank into the floor of the mine, the soft and yielding materials of which rose into and filled up the excavations until the whole became a solid mass. They were productive of great expense and inconvenience, contracting the air-ways, and shattering the stoppings built to guide the ventilating current. At times the movement extended to the surface. It is related that on one occasion when the congregation was assembled in the church at Long Benton, a few pieces of plaster were observed to fall from the ceiling. Noticing a feeling of uneasiness spreading among the congregation, the clergyman announced that it was "only a creep." His flock was however little quieted by the assurance, and lost no time in making good their escape to the outside of the church, leaving their worthy pastor reiterating the announcement that it was "only a creep; only a creep."

The only expedient known for arresting the progress of these movements was the bold one of removing several rows of pillars in front of it, and thus inducing a complete break of the overlying strata; a proceeding analogous to that employed in checking the advance of a prairie fire by burning up the vegetation in its path.

It was now customary to sink the deeper pits of a larger diameter than formerly, viz., from twelve to fourteen feet; and they were usually divided by wooden partitions, or *brattices*, into two, three, or four compartments, so as to admit of pumping, ventilating, and drawing coal, being all carried on by means of a single pit. The arrangement, however, was a highly objectionable one, inasmuch as in the event of an explosion taking place the brattices were blown to pieces, and falling to the bottom of the shaft cut off all communication with the surface and prevented access to the workings. They were also liable to be set on fire by the ventilating furnace; an accident likely to result in the death of all in the mine if no other outlet existed.

The evils of the existing system of mining were nowhere more severely felt than in the deep, extensive, and fiery collieries on the Tyne, the management of which Mr. Buddle was called upon to undertake. Owing to creeps which took place in some portions of Wallsend and Hebburn Collieries the ventilation was deranged, and the air-currents loaded with inflammable gas, to such a degree as to necessitate the discontinuance of ventilation by means of furnaces. Accordingly between the years 1807 and 1810 Mr. Buddle attempted to employ various kinds of ventilating power in lieu of the furnace. Of these the *steam ventilator* was an apparatus for discharging steam into the upcast pit a few fathoms below the surface, the heat of which rarefied the air and produced a ventilating current. Another expedient was the *hot cylinder*, which consisted of a cast-iron cylinder fixed in a brick furnace, and completely enveloped in flame; and the mouth of the upcast pit being covered up, the air-current was passed through this cylinder and escaped by a chimney built for the purpose. The *air-pump* was also tried, having a piston five feet square and a stroke of eight feet, and was capable of exhausting 5,000 or 6,000 cubic feet of air per minute, at a velocity of from twenty to thirty strokes. The preceding appliances, however, though useful as temporary expedients in cases of difficulty, failed to afford results approaching in efficiency to a furnace placed at the bottom of the upcast shaft.

Mr. Buddle now turned his attention to the minimising of the dangers connected with the use of the furnace, and soon succeeded in devising a number of excellent improvements whereby many of the most serious difficulties attending the working of the deeper collieries were happily obviated. This he effected by subdividing the workings and ventilation into a series of independent systems.

Instead of following out one uniform and homogeneous plan, as had been the practice heretofore in all the collieries of the north, Mr. Buddle apportioned the area to be worked into a number of divisions, or *panels*, separated from each other by ribs, or barriers, of solid coal. This he termed "panel-work." The origin of the new arrangement is described by him as follows :—

"Though the removing or robbing of the pillars left in the first working had long been practised in shallow collieries yielding little inflammable gas, it had not originally been contemplated in the deeper and more fiery collieries, the pillars of which were accordingly made only of such strength as was deemed necessary to support the superincumbent strata, and were intended to be permanently sacrificed, it being impossible to maintain the ventilation in an efficient state after the removal of the pillars had been commenced. About the year 1795, however, when the Main Coal at Walker Colliery was exhausted with the exception of the pillars, a scheme was devised by Mr. Thomas Barnes, the viewer of the colliery, for working off a portion of the pillars without either disturbing the ventilation or bringing a creep on the colliery. This was effected by dividing the workings into small areas, of from ten to twelve acres, around which artificial barriers were constructed by packing up all the excavated passages for a breadth of forty or fifty yards. By this means any creep which might take place in the inclosed district was prevented from extending to the surrounding pillars, and the produce of coal obtained from the seam was increased from 39 to 54 per cent."

The above arrangement having proved successful at Walker was adopted soon after at the adjoining colliery of Bigge's Main; and the same plan was pursued at Wallsend, when the robbing of the pillars commenced in 1810.

Mr. Barnes's scheme, however, was only an expedient adapted to pre-existing conditions, and it occurred to Mr. Buddle that a great improvement upon it might be effected by dividing a colliery, in the course of the first working, into districts, or *panels*, surrounded on all sides by barriers of solid coal, and thus to obviate the necessity of subsequently constructing the artificial ones employed in Mr. Barnes's system. This course Mr. Buddle at once adopted in the G pit at Wallsend, which was a separate winning unconnected with the rest of the colliery; and here it was that *panel-work*, as it was termed, was first introduced in the year 1810.

By the adoption of panel-work an effectual check was put to the spread of creeps, the primary object of the arrangement; but other benefits were obtained at the same time; as for example the facility with which accidental fires in the workings could be extinguished by the insertion of air-tight dams in the few openings through the barrier.

Coincidently with the subdivision of the workings

into panels Mr. Buddle effected a great improvement in the ventilation of collieries by dividing the ventilating current. This improvement also was first introduced in the Wallsend G pit in 1810. Mr. Buddle had thought of the arrangement some time previously, but was deterred from putting it into practice because it was not in accordance with the views of many of the old and experienced pitmen, who entertained "a horror of dividing a current of air, inasmuch as that each division, or split, would weaken the principal current." As first applied by Mr. Buddle the improvement consisted in the employment of two air-currents instead of one, and was introduced where two downcast pits, or two compartments of the same pit, could be used to discharge their air into one upcast pit. Such was the case at the Wallsend G pit, which was divided into three compartments, two of which were downcast, and the third an upcast pit.

The new system was termed by Mr. Buddle double or *compound ventilation*. In its simplest form two air-currents were employed, which ventilated separate divisions of the workings and were discharged by separate passages into the upcast shaft. In each of the passages leading into the upcast pit furnaces were provided, only one of which was kept burning; the passage in which it was placed being hence termed the *furnace drift*. The other passage was known as the *dumb drift*. The air-current which ventilated the portion of the workings yielding the least quantity of inflammable gas was passed over the burning furnace; the other current, however loaded with impurities, was discharged with safety through the dumb drift without at all coming in contact with fire on its way. In the event of the state of the workings undergoing a reversal the furnace in the dumb drift could be lighted and the other extinguished, in which case the furnace drift became for the time being the dumb drift.

To maintain an equilibrium between the two currents, sham doors, or *regulators*, were provided to check the velocity of the shorter run; and inasmuch as it was frequently necessary to pass the one current over the other, passages termed *crossings* were provided, which were constructed by throwing an arch over the lower air-way and cutting a channel out of the roof for the upper one.

By the introduction of compound ventilation not only was much of the danger previously attending the employment of ventilating furnaces obviated, but many other important advantages were obtained. Numerous doors were dispensed with, and thus one of the most vulnerable points in Spedding's system of ventilation was overcome. No air-current had to travel more than half of the distance formerly necessary; and as more passages were provided the amount of friction was greatly reduced. In addition to this, fresh air being supplied in two streams instead of one, the atmosphere of the mine was rendered much more wholesome; and the impurities contained in even the last of the air immensely lessened. The expedient of throwing open the main doors and extinguishing the furnace, frequently necessary under the old system, had rarely to be resorted to under the new one.

No sooner had the system of compound ventilation been successfully applied in the Wallsend G pit than its use was extended to other parts of the colliery, as well as to the other collieries under Mr. Buddle's care, wherever two or more downcast pits could be made to communicate with one upcast. Before the close of 1813 it had been introduced by him at Percy Main, Hebburn, and Heaton Collieries. With shafts of sufficient area, the number of subdivisions of the ventilating current was found to be capable of indefinite multiplication; and the system underwent great development subsequently in the hands of Mr. Buddle and his contemporaries. Mr. Buddle's system of ventilation is now known as *splitting the air*, and is the system invariably practised in all well-regulated collieries at the present day.

CHAPTER XVI.

INVENTION OF THE SAFETY LAMP.

"What fairer triumph, what brighter extension of the empire of science, has marked the annals of philosophy, than this victory over the swart demon of the mine?"—SURTEES.

MR. BUDDLE'S improvements had introduced a new order of things in the ventilation and working of collieries, but certain other known sources of danger remained for which no remedial measure had yet been thought of. It is true that the risk attendant upon the use of ventilating furnaces had been materially lessened by the invention of the dumb drift, but no improvement had been effected in the methods employed to light the miners at their work. This continued in the same unsatisfactory position as it had been since the days of the elder Spedding.

If the inflammable gas met with in coal mines were discharged into the workings in equable and determinate quantities, and if the ventilating arrangements were at all times in a state of thorough efficiency, it might be possible, by the introduction and proper distribution of sufficient volumes of atmospheric air, to sweep off the gas as fast as it was produced, and so to maintain the mine in a safe condition. But so far from this being the case, the quantity of gas given off from the goaves, or wastes, varies with the varying pressure of the atmosphere; accumulations of gas are liable to be formed through the temporary neglect of a door, or derangement of a stopping; while danger of a still more formidable character arises from *outbursts*, or sudden discharges of large volumes of inflammable gas, which occasionally take place unexpectedly in deep mines, and instantly overpower, for the time being, the strongest ventilation. If from any of these causes the atmosphere of the mine has become explosive, it is obvious that the presence of a single lighted candle or lamp is sufficient to give rise to the most disastrous consequences.

In situations where the use of ordinary lights was inadmissible, owing to the presence or fear of inflammable gas, the steel mill continued to be resorted to; and notwithstanding its known insecurity and the poor flickering light which it afforded, and the great cost with which its use was attended, it was still largely employed at many collieries between 1810 and 1815. At Hebburn Colliery, where the ventilation had been deranged by a creep taking place, as many as one hundred of these machines were in daily use.

The first person to entertain the idea of supplying the coal miners with a better and safer light was Dr. Clanny, a medical gentleman residing in Sunderland. His attention was drawn to the subject by the frequency with which explosions took place at collieries in the neighbourhood, and it occurred to him that some arrangement might be devised for *insulating the miners' lights* so as to prevent them from communicating explosion to the surrounding atmosphere.

Having given much thought to the matter, Dr. Clanny proceeded to put his idea to the test of experiment. His first lamp was constructed about the end of the year 1811. It was a small lamp of strong glass, and shut at the bottom, with the exception of a small opening to admit a tube from the bellows, which he used for throwing in the necessary quantity of air to support the combustion of the candle. He found he could safely insulate the candle in this way, but was told his lamp would never answer, as it was certain to get broken in the mine.

In the course of his experiments, Dr. Clanny tried a lamp insulated by means of valves, but found they would not suit, as the expansive force of an explosion within the lamp threw them open, and allowed a communication to take place with the surrounding atmosphere. At length, in the beginning of the year 1813, he succeeded in constructing a strong form of lamp which was perfectly insulated by the ingenious arrangement of passing the air from the bellows into the lamp through a stratum of water below, while a similar stratum of water above allowed the products of combustion to escape safely at the top. An account of this lamp was communicated by him to the Royal Society, in a paper " On a Steady Light in Coal Mines," read on the 20th of May, 1813.

Dr. Clanny's lamp, however, was useful rather as directing attention to the matter and showing what might be done in the way of providing a greater degree of efficiency and security in the lighting of coal mines. It was highly approved of by many scientific gentlemen, and after various tests had been applied to it to prove its security, it was carried by Dr. Clanny into a dangerous mine at the risk of his life; but the idea was novel, and the lamp being somewhat inconvenient, it did not come into practical use, at least to any extent.

But though Dr. Clanny is entitled to the high merit of being the first to conceive and carrry out the idea of constructing an insulated lamp, he did not long remain alone in this department of invention, the attention of many minds being drawn to the subject soon afterwards by a series of occurrences which we shall proceed to narrate.

On the 25th of May, 1812, an explosion occurred at Brandling Main, or Felling Colliery, near Gateshead-on-Tyne, which was attended with a more appalling loss of life than any like calamity that had ever taken place in the annals of coal-mining. Ninety-two men and boys were destroyed by the blast. This great loss of life was occasioned by the disaster happening at a most inauspicious moment. It is the common custom in the North of England to work the collieries with two shifts or sets of men, and for several reasons it is made a rule that the men of the first shift remain at their working-places until relieved by the arrival of the men of the second shift. Hence, during a short space of time, both sets of men are in the mine at the same moment, and this was unfortunately the case when the above-mentioned explosion took place. Out of one hundred and twenty-one persons who had entered the mine, only thirty-two escaped alive, three of whom died within a few hours after the accident.

The colliery was at this time the property of Messrs. John and William Brandling, Henderson, and Grace, each of whom held a fourth share. It is situated in the parish of Jarrow and Heworth, of which the Rev. J. Hodgson (who afterwards became celebrated as the historian of Northumberland) was the incumbent. As Mr. Hodgson resided at Heworth, this dreadful calamity occurred at his very door, and on him devolved the task of administering the consolations of religion to the bereaved, and of performing the last solemn rites beside the graves of the dead.

Mr. Hodgson was not unacquainted with the details of coal-mining operations. He had lived for a considerable number of years in the Newcastle coal district, and had made frequent descents into the mines. At this time the editors of newspapers avoided publishing accounts of colliery explosions, being afraid of giving offence by doing so. Impressed, however, with the conviction that something further might be done to prevent the recurrence of such calamities, Mr. Hodgson, *contrary to the feelings of the coalowners*, determined to make the circumstances connected with the Felling explosion as widely known as possible, with the hope of rousing the attention of scientific men to investigate the causes of these accidents, and find some mode of preventing them. To this end, for many weeks he continued to write notices, respecting the accident, to the *Newcastle Courant*, and also wrote and published a particular account of it and its consequences, accompanied with a plan of the mine and the mode of ventilating it. This publication (the preface of which is dated 4th January, 1813) was widely circulated; and part of it, unknown to Mr. Hodgson, was inserted in Dr. Thomson's *Annals of Philosophy* for May of the same year.

Among those whose sympathies were excited by the recital of the dangers to which the workers in coal mines were exposed was a Mr. J. J. Wilkinson, a barrister resident in the Temple. During the Long Vacation in 1813 Mr. Wilkinson went to the North of England, and consulted with many of his friends on the matter, which resulted in his determining to call the attention of the public to colliery explosions with a view to the investigation of the whole subject, to see if any remedy could be found. With this object, on the 1st of September, 1813, he published, and sent into Durham and Northumberland, proposals for the establishment of a society for preventing accidents in coal mines. These proposals having come under the notice of the Bishop of Durham, among others, his Lordship wrote to the Rev. Dr. Gray, then Rector of Bishopwearmouth (afterwards Bishop of Bristol), giving him *càrte blanche* to aid in the formation of such a society. A meeting of those interested was accordingly arranged for, and was held at Sunderland on the 1st of October, 1813, when the society was duly instituted and a Committee appointed to carry out the objects contemplated.

In the following month the society issued its first report, which contained a very valuable letter, voluntarily communicated by Mr. Buddle to Sir Ralph Milbanke, the president, in which was given a detailed account of the various systems employed to effect the ventilation of collieries—"the only method we are at present acquainted with," says the writer, "for the prevention of accidents by fire." In concluding his letter,

Mr. Buddle expresses his conviction that any further application of mechanical agency would be ineffectual to prevent explosions in mines exposed to excessive discharges of fire-damp, "and therefore," he says, "conclude that the hopes of this society ever seeing its most desirable object accomplished must rest upon the event of some method being discovered of producing such a chemical change upon carburetted hydrogen gas as to render it innoxious as fast as it is discharged, or as it approaches the neighbourhood of lights. In this view of the subject, it is to scientific men only that we must look up for assistance in providing a cheap and effectual remedy."

It was deemed advisable to apply to Sir Humphry Davy, the distinguished chemist and philosopher, and Mr. Wilkinson accordingly called at the Royal Institution, but found that he was absent in Paris. Mr. Wilkinson then posted a letter to Sir Humphry, but having neglected to pay the foreign postage, it was returned to Mr. Burn, the secretary of the society.

At this time so little expectation was entertained that any means could be devised likely to prevent explosions in collieries, that the object of the society was regarded as chimerical and visionary. Amidst much difficulty and discouragement, however, and a perpetual harass by the offer of impracticable schemes, they persevered in their meetings, though their humane efforts were for a considerable period attended with little success.

In the meantime colliery accidents continued to occur from time to time. A second explosion took place at Felling Colliery on the 24th of December, 1813, occasioning the loss of twenty-three lives. In 1814 explosions occurred: at Percy Main Colliery, on the 15th of April, with the loss of four lives; at Hebburn Colliery, on the 12th of August, with the loss of eleven lives; and at Seafield Colliery, on the 9th of September, with the loss of four lives. On the 3rd of May, 1815, the great inundation took place at Heaton Colliery, causing a loss of seventy-five lives; on the 2nd of June, Newbottle Colliery exploded, with the loss of fifty-seven lives; and on the 27th of the same month, Sheriff Hill Colliery exploded, with the loss of eleven lives.

Ever since the occurrence of the first explosion at Felling, accounts of similar accidents which took place were regularly forwarded to, and published in, Dr. Thomson's *Annals of Philosophy*, and thus the attention of the scientific world was kept alive to the matter. The idea of the practicability of employing insulated lights, which Dr. Clanny had never ceased to advocate, was gradually gaining ground. In his *Elements of Chemical Science*, published in June, 1815, Mr. Murray, a lecturer on chemistry, proposed the use of an airtight lamp, which was to be supplied with air through a tube extending downwards to the floor of the mine. Lamps on this principle were actually constructed by Mr. Brandling, and Dr. John Murray, of Edinburgh, during the summer or autumn of 1815; but as they presupposed the existence of determinate strata in the air of a mine, which is not the case, they were inapplicable to the purpose intended.

A correspondence regarding insulated lights for miners was also commenced in the *Morning Chronicle* by Mr. J. H. H. Holmes (author of a treatise on the coal mines of Durham and Northumberland), the first letter being dated 12th July, 1815. Mr. Holmes was desirous to know, from motives of humanity, whether Dr. Clanny's insulated lamp had been in use in any of the collieries where explosions had recently occurred. This led to a series of letters between Dr. Clanny and Mr. Holmes, which were published successively for a number of weeks.

We have seen that the first endeavour of the Sunderland Society to obtain the assistance of Sir Humphry Davy had proved abortive, owing to his absence on the Continent. In the close of the summer of 1815 it was again resolved to apply to him, and a letter was accordingly despatched to London by Dr. Gray, the Chairman of the Committee, who was generally acquainted with Sir Humphry. Dr. Gray's letter followed Sir Humphry into Scotland, whither he had gone on a visit to Lord Somerville, at Melrose. In his reply, dated 3rd August, Sir Humphry expresses the great satisfaction it will give him if his chemical knowledge can be of any use in an inquiry so interesting to humanity, and begs Dr.

Gray to assure the Committee of his readiness to cooperate with them in any experiments or investigations on the subject. He offers at the same time to visit the mines, should it be thought desirable for him to do so.

It having been arranged that Sir Humphry should visit the coal district on his way south, he arrived in Newcastle on the 23rd or 24th of August, where he was waited upon at the Turk's Head by Mr. Hodgson, who laid before him all the printed information he knew of respecting the ventilating and lighting of coal mines—Sir Humphry entering at once with ardour into the subject. They then proceeded together to Mr. Buddle's house at Wallsend.

Mr. Hodgson had, among other things, communicated to Sir Humphry a theory which he had been led to form regarding the source of the inflammable gas in coal mines, by some experiments which he had made, viz., that it existed in the coal itself. Little was known then on this subject, though various hypotheses had been suggested. Some thought that it arose from the decomposition of the water in the mines; others from the decomposition of the coal or of the iron pyrites contained it. At Mr. Buddle's house, after much general conversation on the subject of the safe lighting of mines, Sir Humphry took up in his own hand a bucket of fresh coal and said: "With this I will try Mr. Hodgson's experiment on coal gas." Carrying it into Mr. Buddle's dining-room, he asked for a bucket of water, and having put some coal into it, and stirred it round several times that no air might remain, he struck a heavy poker with all his strength on the coal, shattering it into several pieces, whereupon numerous bubbles rose through the water. On this Sir Humphry remarked that Mr. Hodgson's experiments were certainly correct and interesting. The only other point he wished to ascertain, he said, was the minimum of light with which the colliers could see to work. This was exhibited to him by procuring a steel mill and "playing" it in a dark place.

From the first Sir Humphry entertained a sanguine hope of being able to help the miners in their difficulties. Mr. Buddle took the opposite view:—

"I explained to him," he says, "as well as I was able, the nature of our fiery mines, and that the great desideratum was a light that could be safely used in an explosive mixture. I had not the slightest idea myself of ever seeing such a thing accomplished. . . . . Just as we were parting he looked at me and said, 'I think I can do something for you.' Thinking it was too much ever to be achieved, I gave him a look of incredulity; at the moment it was beyond my comprehension. However, smiling, he said, 'Do not despair; I think I can do something for you in a very short time.'"

From Mr. Buddle's house, Sir Humphry and Mr. Hodgson proceeded to Coaly Hill, to examine a geological phenomenon mentioned by the latter, which Sir Humphry had expressed a strong desire to see. This consisted of an intrusive dyke of whin, or basalt, on the sides of which the coal had been charred for some distance by the heat of the whin when first injected in a molten state.

Having inspected several parts of the dyke with great interest, Sir Humphry and Mr. Hodgson went to Hebburn Hall, where they had been invited by Mr. Ellison (who was a very kind friend of Mr. Hodgson's) to dine and spend the night.

On the following morning Sir Humphry proceeded to Dr. Gray's, at Bishopwearmouth, and in the course of the day, accompanied by Dr. Gray's eldest son, he called at Dr. Clanny's house, being desirous to see Dr. Clanny and his insulated lamp. Dr. Clanny was not at home; neither was he at home when Sir Humphry called a second time on the same day.

Hearing of Sir Humphry's visits on his return home, Dr. Clanny, being much engaged at the time, took the lamp in his carriage, and calling at Dr. Gray's, left it for the inspection of Sir Humphry, who remained at the rectory overnight. On the following morning Sir Humphry had an interview with Dr. Clanny, who had been invited to breakfast at Dr. Gray's, but did not arrive till after the meal was over, when he found Sir Humphry engaged in making some experiments with his lamp.

Leaving Bishopwearmouth, Sir Humphry paid visits to Auckland Castle, Egglestone, Rokeby, and Harwood

House, remaining at the latter place till the 29th or 30th of September.

On the 29th of September Sir Humphry wrote to Mr. Hodgson requesting him to send him a quantity of fire-damp from a blower. Six wine-bottles were accordingly filled from a strong blower of gas coming from a dyke in Hebburn Colliery, and were transmitted to Sir Humphry on the 5th of October. In a letter dated 15th October, Sir Humphry acknowledged the receipt of the fire-damp, and announced to Mr. Hodgson that his investigations were progressing well. "My experiments," he says, "are going on successfully, and I hope in a few days to send you an account of them; I am going to be fortunate far beyond my expectations."

The progress of Sir Humphry Davy in the new path of discovery which he had entered upon was as rapid as it was brilliant, and from time to time he communicated the results of his researches to his friends in the north and to the scientific circles in London.

On the 19th of October, in a letter to Mr. Hodgson, *he announces an entirely new method of insulating lights.* "I have already discovered," he says, "that explosive mixtures of mine-damp will not pass through small apertures or tubes; and that if a lamp or lanthorn be made air-tight on the sides, and furnished with apertures to admit the air, it will not communicate flame to the outward atmosphere."

On the 25th of October, Sir Humphry communicated the progress of his discoveries to the Chemical Club of London.

On the 30th of October he wrote simultaneously to Dr. Gray and Mr. Hodgson, giving an account of his discoveries with considerable detail, and describing three forms of insulated lamps. In these communications he states, among other things, that—

"Atmospherical air, when rendered impure by the combustion of a candle, but in which the candle will still burn, will not explode the gas from the mines; and when a lamp or candle is made to burn in a close vessel, having apertures only above and below, an explosive mixture of gas admitted merely enlarges the light and gradually extinguishes it without explosion. Again, the gas mixed in any proportion with common air I have discovered will not explode in small tubes, the diameter of which is less than one-eighth of an inch, or even a larger tube, if there is a mechanical force urging the gas through the tube."

The above communications were not intended to be made public at this stage.

"I consider this at present as a *private* communication," says Sir Humphry in his letter to Dr. Gray. "I wish you to examine the lamps I have had constructed, before you give any account of my labours to the committee. I have never received so much pleasure from the result of any of my chemical labours; for I trust the cause of humanity will gain something by it."

The letter sent to Mr. Hodgson was copied by several professional men of the neighbourhood on the 2nd of

November. [Perhaps Mr. Matthias Dunn, who procured the fire-damp, may have been one of them. He gives an extract from it in his *View of the Coal Trade*, but by some error has dated the letter 15th instead of 30th October.] Mr. Hodgson tells us that he records this fact merely to show that Sir Humphry's discoveries were known at this time to several persons in the Newcastle district besides himself. He did not imagine that any of the gentlemen who copied his letter made an improper use of it.

In an oration delivered on the 4th of November at the foundation of the college of the Royal Institution, Mr. Butler alluded, in terms of exultation, to the process discovered "within these few weeks" by Sir H. Davy, whereby the fire-damp of coal mines had been absolutely subdued.

On the 9th of November, Sir Humphry read his first paper to the Royal Society relative to the progress of his discoveries. It is entitled, "On the fire-damp of coal mines, and on methods of lighting the mines so as to prevent its explosion." As this paper is published in the *Philosophical Transactions*, it is unnecessary to enter into any account of the innumerable delicate experiments made by Sir Humphry before he succeeded in producing lamps which were at once safe and gave a good light. It may be remarked, however, that the results achieved were arrived at by processes which could only have been pursued by an individual conversant with all the resources of chemical science, and with every appliance at his command, leaving out of view altogether the rare creative genius of Sir Humphry Davy.

We have entered with considerable detail into the dates at which the various announcements of the progress of Sir Humphry Davy's discoveries were made, on account of the claim to priority of invention which was shortly afterwards put forward by Mr. R. W. Brandling on behalf of George Stephenson, who at this time was an engineer at Killingworth Colliery, near Newcastle-on-Tyne. It is perfectly clear that for some time, at all events, Sir Humphry and Mr. Stephenson were devoting their energies simultaneously to the invention of an insulated lamp on entirely different lines. The first occasion on which a *rencontre* took place between their respective lamps was at a public meeting of the coal-trade held at Newcastle-on-Tyne on the 10th of November.

It will be remembered that Sir Humphry Davy addressed letters containing an account of his discoveries to Dr. Gray and Mr. Hodgson on the 30th of October, and that these communications were intended to be kept private. Mr. Hodgson, however, having seen a notice of Sir Humphry's labours in the public newspapers, considered it no longer necessary to maintain any reserve, and on his own responsibility attended the above-mentioned meeting and read to the coal-owners the communication which he had received. The reading of the paper appeared to excite considerable interest. Mr. Hodgson was not aware at the time that Sir Humphry Davy had any rival in the field, but after he had read the paper, some gentlemen from the neighbourhood of Killingworth, among whom was Mr. R. Lambert, made mention of Mr. Stephenson's lamp, which Mr. Hodgson then heard of for the first time. We shall now, therefore, proceed to endeavour to elucidate the origin and progress of Mr. Stephenson's efforts to invent an insulated lamp.

In the summer of 1815 Mr. Stephenson, in his capacity of engineer, being engaged in setting up some machinery in the Killingworth pit, frequently set fire to a blower of gas which he passed on his way underground to and from his work. He was expostulated with by several pitmen regarding the danger of this proceeding, but excused himself by stating "generally" that he thought he could make it useful to preserve men's lives. Having discovered that, by holding a number of lighted candles on the windward side of the blower, he could extinguish its flame by the "burnt air" proceeding from them, he was led to form a theory on which he thought a safety-lamp might be constructed. It was, "that if a lamp could be made to contain the burnt air above the flame, and to permit the fire-damp to come in below in small quantity, to be burnt as it came in, the burnt air would prevent the passing of explosion upwards, and the velocity of the current from below would also prevent its passing downwards."

This theory he communicated to Mr. Nicholas Wood "about or before the month of August." No steps, however, were taken to carry out the idea till the beginning of the month of October, at which time a plan was made by Mr. Wood from Mr. Stephenson's directions; and the lamp was ordered from Mr. Hogg, a tinman in Newcastle, "most probably as early as the 2nd, but certainly before the 7th of October." It was at first intended to supply air to the lamp through a tube in the bottom $\frac{1}{4}$ of an inch in diameter, but on its being represented by Mr. Hogg that it probably would not burn, the tube was made $\frac{1}{2}$ an inch in diameter, and a slide was attached in order to lessen it if necessary. At the same time a glass for the lamp was ordered at the Northumberland Glass-House. It was conical in shape and open at the top.

The lamp was completed and delivered to Mr. Stephenson on the 21st of October, and on the evening of the same day was tried at the blower in Killingworth Colliery. It was found that when the slide was so far shut that the lamp burnt "but feebly" in good air, when exposed to the current of the blower, "within a few inches of the mouth," the flame of the lamp increased in size, and then went out, without communicating explosion to the gas outside; but when in this condition, the lamp was easily put out by motion.

Mr. Stephenson's biographer has constructed a "pretty story" about the trial of this lamp, in which he states, with considerable emphasis, that the very first experiment with it was made by Mr. Stephenson in the mine at the risk of his own life. Mr. Wood, however, who was present, explains that the danger was not quite so great as represented by Mr. Smiles. "At most," he says, "an explosion might have burnt the hands of the operator, but would not extend a few feet from the blower."

Whatever was proved by the trials to which the lamp was put, it was found that the tube and slide arrangement was a failure. If it was safe at all, it was only when the flame of the lamp was reduced to such a degree as to be practically valueless, as it could not bear being carried about. It was consequently determined to make alterations; and, as Mr. Stephenson conceived that the cause of the lamp going out (when moved quickly, he says) was owing to the "burnt air" hanging about the flame, he determined to apply three smaller tubes instead of one large one, and to place them round the flame and point them towards it, in order to dispel this air. The lamp was accordingly forthwith intrusted to a Mr. Matthews, a tinman in Newcastle, who made the alterations; but they were of such a trivial description that the transaction was not entered in his books, and no particulars were preserved by him either of the date or of the size of the tubes. They are stated, however, to have been made of such a size as the experiments with the slide had determined to be the dimensions of safety—the safety, we presume, ascribed to "the velocity of the current from below."

The altered lamp was delivered to Mr. Stephenson on the 4th of November, and tried in Killingworth Colliery on the same day. The accounts of the trial are somewhat laconic. Mr. Stephenson says it was "found safe." Mr. Wood tells us that it was "found to burn better than the other, but still not well; still, however, the explosion did not pass downwards." The overman states that Stephenson thought, and he agreed with him, "that the altered lamp burnt better than the former;" also that the lamp was tried in a "very foul" place, and the effect was the same as before; the flame increased and then went out.

Whether the tests which were applied to the altered lamp can be regarded as conclusive evidence of its safety is perhaps questionable. It is scarcely probable that either Mr. Stephenson or his companions knew at this time that pure fire-damp extinguishes lights, or were acquainted with the proportions of gas and air which form the most explosive mixture. Again, was the lamp proof against passing explosion *upwards?* However this may be, there appears to have been a general consensus of opinion as to its deficient burning powers. Even Mr. Stephenson was disappointed with it. "It did not entirely answer my expectations," he says; nor is this surprising, inasmuch as, according to his *theory*, his lamp was to *burn* among fire-damp, whereas it did exactly the reverse.

This lamp was never exhibited outside of Killingworth, but two subsequent sets of experiments were made with it there which are worthy of note. We are told that "on the 17th of November it was tried at Killingworth office, with inflammable air, before Richard Lambert, Esq.; and on the 24th of November before R. W. Brandling, Esq., C. J. Brandling, Esq., and Mr. Murray;" but that at the latter date Mr. Stephenson had a new lamp in the hands of the manufacturer.

What transpired at Killingworth office on the 17th of November we do not know; it is possible that neither Sir Humphry Davy, nor his lamps with apertures above and below, were ever mentioned. Neither do we know whether the notice of Sir Humphry Davy's discoveries which appeared in the *Newcastle Chronicle* on the 18th of November was seen by Mr. Stephenson. One thing, however, appears to be pretty certain, and that is that at this particular juncture a new light burst in upon Mr. Stephenson, and that he instantly set about constructing a new lamp, which differed in several essential particulars from his three-tube lamp. The plan of the new lamp was not drawn by Mr. Wood, but by a "Mr. Henry Smith, clerk to Robert Watson, plumber in Newcastle." It was ordered on the 19th or 20th of November, and was made and delivered to Mr. Stephenson in a few days.

In the new lamp the air was admitted through a series of apertures below, and it escaped through apertures above. This lamp was tried in the Killingworth Mine on the 30th of November, "and found to be perfectly safe and to burn extremely well." On the 5th of December it was exhibited and experimented upon, with fire-damp, before a general meeting of the Literary and Philosophical Society of Newcastle-on-Tyne. We are told that at this meeting Mr. Wood attempted to explain the *rationale* of the lamp, but was unable to do so; whereupon Mr. Stephenson stepped forward and described it "down to its minutest details." The account given by a gentleman who was present at the meeting (Mr. J. H. H. Holmes) is somewhat different—

"Mr. Stephenson," he says, "undoubtedly claims great merit if the invention produced was from his own genius. . . . . The principle of this lamp is its being supplied with air through small perforations at the bottom, which, when in pure atmospheric air, enables the light to burn something similar to the radiance of a rushlight. . . . . In regard to this lantern having been tried in a mine six weeks previous to its appearance at the meeting, I must express some doubts, as it certainly did not wear the appearance of so old a practitioner, and as Mr. Stephenson appeared totally ignorant of the manner in which the air and gases operated upon the light. Nothing was heard or said of it previous to the private meeting before spoken of (held on the 28th of November), which was exclusively for the purpose of taking into consideration the methods of lighting collieries."

There is a lamp now in the possession of the Literary and Philosophical Society of Newcastle-on-Tyne, which is stated to be the identical lamp exhibited at the above meeting. If it be so, it is not in the same condition as it then was; *e.g.*, the lamp exhibited had a conical glass, and no trimmer: the lamp now in the possession of the society has a cylindrical glass, and the Davy trimmer.

After what has been already stated, it seems unnecessary to enter into the question of priority of invention. It must be evident, we imagine, that in every particular Mr. Stephenson was anticipated by Sir Humphry Davy; while any improvements subsequently made, based upon the *chemical* discoveries of Davy, however ingenious and useful they may be, cannot be regarded as original inventions.

The discovery which Sir Humphry Davy had made, that explosion would not pass through small apertures and tubes, was only a stepping-stone to still higher achievements; and before the close of the year 1815 he gave to the world the *wire-gauze* lamp. This was the last, the most splendid, the crowning triumph of his labours—the "metallic tissue, permeable to light and air, and impermeable to flame."

The first "Davy lamps"—as the gauze lamps were

named after their illustrious inventor—were sent to the North of England in the beginning of January, 1816, and, after a few preliminary experiments, were tried in Hebburn Colliery by Mr. Matthias Dunn and the Rev. J. Hodgson, with the most excellent results.

By no one was the invention more eagerly welcomed than by Mr. Buddle; no one was a better judge of its inestimable value. "I first tried it," he says, "in an explosive mixture on the surface, and then took it into a mine; and, to my astonishment and delight, it is impossible for me to express my feelings at the time when I first suspended the lamp in the mine, and saw it red-hot; if it had been a monster destroyed, I could not have felt more exultation than I did. I said to those around me, 'We have at last subdued this monster.'"

A few months later Sir Humphry Davy accompanied Mr. Buddle into some of the fiery mines of the north to see his lamp in actual use. "Sir Humphry was delighted," says Mr. Buddle, "and I was overwhelmed with feelings of gratitude to that great genius which had produced it."

Mr. Buddle remonstrated with Sir Humphry for not securing the invention by a patent, from which he might have derived an income of five or ten thousand a year. "The reply of this great and noble-minded man," he says, was "'No, my good friend, I never thought of such a thing; my sole object was to serve the cause of humanity; and if I have succeeded, I am amply rewarded in the gratifying reflection of having done so.'"

No sooner had the immense value of the Davy lamp become manifest, than the coal-owners determined to present Sir Humphry with a substantial token of their admiration and gratitude. To this Mr. R. W. Brandling demurred, bringing forward the claims of Mr. Stephenson, and requesting that an investigation should first be made to ascertain who was the real inventor. This proposal was submitted to a meeting of the coal-owners and negatived. The same meeting, however, voted one hundred guineas to Mr. Stephenson, as an acknowledgment of his labours in the same direction.

The presentation to Sir Humphry Davy was made at a dinner held at the Queen's Head, Newcastle, on the 25th of September, 1817, Mr. J. G. Lambton presiding. It consisted of a service of plate worth 2,500*l.*

Mr. Stephenson's friends, being dissatisfied, commenced a subscription on his behalf. The amount collected, added to the previous sum voted by the coal-owners, reached the handsome total of about 800*l.* This, together with a silver tankard, was presented to Mr. Stephenson by Mr. Brandling, at a public dinner held in the Assembly Rooms, Newcastle, in January, 1818.

The claims of Dr. Clanny were long overlooked. He received the gold and silver medals of the Society of

Arts; but it was not till as late as 1846 that steps were taken to procure for him some public acknowledgment of his labours in the cause of humanity in connection with colliery explosions. An appeal having been made on his behalf, a purse of gold was collected, which together with a silver salver, was presented to him at the Athenæum, Sunderland, on the 3rd of February, 1848.

The invention of the safety-lamp was regarded by Dr. Gray as a sufficient reason for dissolving the Sunderland Society for the Prevention of Accidents in Mines.

The share which the Rev. J. Hodgson had had in the steps which led to the invention of the safety-lamp was no small one. It was he who, braving the displeasure of the affluent Brandlings, had vividly portrayed and laid before the public eye, in his little pamphlet on the Felling explosion, the awful spectacle presented by a colliery devastated by "whirlwinds of tempestuous fire," and aroused the attention of the humane to the perils to which the workers in fiery mines were exposed. The assistance he had given in forwarding the invention afforded him some solace even in his last illness.

Sir Humphry Davy in after life always dwelt with peculiar satisfaction and delight upon the invention of his safety-lamp. "I value it," he used to say, "more than anything I ever did. It was the result of a great deal of investigation and labour;

..., if my directions be only attended to, it will save the lives of thousands of poor labourers. I never was more affected than by a written address which I received from the working colliers, when I was in the North, thanking me, in behalf of themselves and their families, for the preservation of their lives." He used also to exhibit to his friends with great delight the service of plate which had been presented to him.

Not only has the safety-lamp been instrumental in saving thousands of lives, but it has also enabled untold millions of tons of coal to be rescued from the bowels of the earth, which without its aid would have been irrevocably lost. It rendered possible the entire removal of the pillars of coal, great part of which was formerly left underground in fiery mines. It led to the re-opening of many collieries which had been abandoned after having been worked out as far as was practicable by means of candles and steel mills. Walker Colliery, which had been abandoned in 1811, was re-opened in 1818 by the aid of the Davy lamp, and has continued working to this day. Great part of the formerly relinquished workings in Wallsend, Willington, Percy Main, Hebburn, Jarrow, Elswick, Benwell, &c., as well as several collieries on the river Wear, were recovered and resumed work by its aid.

The introduction of the safety-lamp did not put an end to colliery explosions; though few indeed are traceable to it, notwithstanding the many thousands of wire-gauze lamps, of various forms, which subsequently came into daily use. Difficulties there are even with its aid; but, in the case of deep mining, what vastly greater, what insuperable difficulties would have existed, had science not armed the miners with the wonderful insulated lamp, which warns them of the presence of their invisible enemy, and protects them from its power.

The dates cited in the above narrative can, we think, be established beyond the possibility of controversy. It is perhaps almost unnecessary to remark that both Dr. Clanny and Mr. Stephenson subsequently adopted the Davy wire gauze in their lamps, but for which vital improvement they would long since have been laid aside.

CHAPTER XVII.

EXTENDED USE OF THE STEAM-ENGINE; THE LOCOMOTIVE; STEAMBOATS.—INTRODUCTION OF GAS-LIGHTING.

> " Soon shall thy arm, unconquer'd Steam ! afar
> Drag the slow barge, or drive the rapid car."
> —DARWIN.

WE have seen that the chief use to which the steam-engine was put for a long period subsequent to the date of its first invention was to draw water from coal and other mines; then it came to be applied indirectly to draw the coal out of the pits through the medium of the double water-wheel; and soon after the invention of the double-acting engine by Watt it began to come into general use applied directly to the shaft of the drum, or rope-roll, and quickly superseded the previous circuitous arrangement. The last of the double water-wheels employed drawing coal in the North of England were at Chopwell Colliery, and the A pit, Greenside, near Ryton; one of which was abandoned in 1800, and the other in 1808.

In the beginning of the present century a further extension of the use of the steam-engine began to be thought of. At this time the conveyance of coal on railways was performed entirely by horses, excepting in cases where conditions existed favourable to the employment of self-acting incline-planes, when the loaded waggons in descending were made to haul up the ascending empty ones. Hence the railways were made merely of sufficient strength to bear the weight of the loaded coal-waggons. On most of them wooden rails were still used, but the employment of cast-iron rails was making steady progress; and in a few cases light bars of malleable iron had been applied on the top of wooden rails with good results. An early railway of the latter description was constructed at Alloa Collieries, on the Frith of Forth, in 1785. The wooden foundation was of a substantial character, consisting of broad sleepers about a foot apart, to which were secured the rails, four inches square, in the form known as the "double-way," there being both an upper and an under rail employed. On the top of the upper rail a light bar of malleable iron was laid, $1\frac{3}{4}$ths of an inch in breadth, and $\frac{3}{4}$ths of an inch in thickness. Light waggons were used, with cast-iron wheels, twenty-seven inches in diameter, and carrying thirty hundredweight of coal; a horse's load consisting of three such waggons. This railway was found to be very solid and durable, and for a number of years was acknowledged to be "the most complete in Britain."

Light malleable-iron rails were also applied at Walbottle Colliery, near Newcastle-on-Tyne, about 1805, but being narrow, they were found to cut the periphery of the waggon wheels, in consequence of which they were subsequently taken up. At Lord Carlisle's colliery, on Tindale Fell, rails of this material gave more satisfaction, being laid down in 1808, and after having been in use for a period of sixteen years they "then appeared very little worse."

But during the first quarter of the present century when iron rails were employed they were almost invariably of cast-iron. They were usually about four feet in length, and of various sections; and were dovetailed together at the joints in several different ways.

At the very commencement of the century a combination of circumstances occurred favourable to the application of the steam-engine to the haulage of coal-waggons on railways. Watt's patent for the double-acting engine had then expired; the steam-engine entered on a new phase of its history when Trevithick discarded the condensing apparatus, and brought out his high-pressure engine; while to this was added the gradual improvement of railways, which was going forward in virtue of the substitution of iron for wood in their *matériel*. Thus it happens that almost simultaneously projects were started for applying the steam-engine to the haulage of railway-waggons, both in the form of travelling engines, or locomotives, dragging the waggons behind them, and of fixed engines hauling with ropes: Trevithick being the first to attempt the former system in South Wales, and Curr the latter in the North of England.

As early as the year 1802 far-seeing individuals had begun to speculate upon the "great national importance" which the locomotive engine (patented in this year by Trevithick and Vivian) might eventually attain to, but many difficulties had to be surmounted before it began to achieve any measure of success. The attempts to employ it on common roads ended in complete failure. On railways for a time it hardly fared much better, chiefly on account of the weakness of the rails. At first a single cylinder and fly-wheel were employed; but though the engine was equal in strength to many horses, its great weight caused it to be constantly breaking the cast-iron rails, while its great strength was too much for the coupling chains between the waggons, which continually gave way. These discouragements caused Trevithick to abandon the locomotive which he applied on the

Merthyr Tydvil railway in 1804,[1] after making only a few trips over the line.

It was doubtless the apprehension of similar difficulties that led Mr. Blackett, the proprietor of Wylam Colliery, near Newcastle-on-Tyne, to give up the project he had entertained of applying one of Trevithick's locomotives to haul the coal-waggons on the railway between his pits and his staiths at Lemington. A locomotive was actually built for him at Gateshead-on-Tyne, in 1805, but it never left the works. After being exhibited to a number of gentlemen, on a temporary railway laid down in the foundry-yard, it was taken off its wheels and converted into a stationary engine.

More success was achieved at first in applying the steam-engine to haul with ropes, especially in cases where a double slope could be arranged for, as an engine placed at the summit served the double purpose of hauling up and lowering both the loaded and empty trains. The first to employ fixed engines in hauling waggons was Mr. Curr, who, in 1805, applied one to raise the waggons from the valley at Birtley, near Gateshead, to the high grounds at Black Fell. This was immediately followed by other schemes of a similar

---

[1] In 1802 the Coalbrookdale Company constructed a locomotive for their railways, but we have no information as to the amount of success attending its working.

character; and about the same time fixed engines began to be employed underground in hauling the coal from dip workings.

Horses continued to be used on level railways, especially such as had a slight fall in favour of the loaded waggons. Not unfrequently several different systems were in use on different parts of the same line—self-acting inclines for single slopes where available, fixed engines for double slopes, and horses on level parts of the road.

Mr. Blackett's railway at Wylam was nearly level, and was entirely worked by horses at considerable cost. Up till the year 1808 it was laid with wooden rails, but at this time he reconstructed it, taking up the wooden rails and laying down cast-iron plate-rails. This step was doubtless taken with a view to the employment of a locomotive engine upon it—a project which he seems to have keep steadily in view though he did not carry it out in 1805. Having renewed the railway he wrote to Trevithick, in 1809, on the subject of a locomotive, the patent for which, held by Trevithick and Vivian, had still seven years to run. In his reply Trevithick stated that he was engaged in other pursuits, and having declined the business could render no assistance. Mr. Blackett's project thus received another check.

An ingenious arrangement for employing the locomotive engine in the haulage of coal-waggons on light railways was invented and patented by Mr. John Blenkinsop in 1811. Blenkinsop was a native of Walker, a village situated about two miles to the east of Newcastle-on-Tyne. He was a cousin and pupil of Mr. Thomas Barnes, the viewer of Walker Colliery and the pits belonging to the Brandling family. On the death of Barnes in 1801, or shortly afterwards, Blenkinsop was appointed viewer of the collieries of J. C. Brandling, Esq., at Middleton, near Leeds. These collieries were connected with the town of Leeds by a railway three or four miles in length, on which the coal waggons were conveyed by horses. Having conceived that the haulage of the coal might be effected more economically by means of a locomotive engine, Blenkinsop devised a scheme for the purpose. His invention consisted in the use of a rack-rail, fixed in the centre of the railway, or forming part of the rails on one side; and the locomotive was arranged to drive a pinion wheel working in the rack-rail, thus propelling itself and the load attached to it. The application of the rack enabled a comparatively light engine to haul a heavy train of waggons.

Blenkinsop employed the then celebrated firm of engineers, Messrs. Fenton, Murray, and Wood, to construct locomotive engines for him. His engines were provided with *two* steam cylinders working cranks at right angles to each other. This was a great improvement on Trevithick's engine, a regular and steady action being obtainable from it without the use of a cumbersome fly-wheel.

The first of Blenkinsop's engines commenced working on the railway from Middleton Collieries to Leeds in June, 1812. Thousands of people assembled to witness the trial of the new and strange machine, which was "crowned with complete success." From this time Leeds was regularly supplied with coal by means of the steam locomotive.

Regarding his engines and their performances Blenkinsop stated, in reply to Sir John Sinclair, that an engine with two eight-inch cylinders weighed five tons, and drew twenty-seven waggons, weighing ninety-four tons, on a dead level, at three and a half miles per hour, or fifteen tons up an ascent of two inches in the yard (1 in 18); when lightly loaded it travelled at ten miles an hour; did the work of sixteen horses in twelve hours, and cost 400*l.*

Blenkinsop's locomotive was a success from the first, and established the fact that the haulage of waggons on level railways might be performed more economically by steam-engines than by horses. It was the most efficient of the early locomotives, but there were several obstacles in the way of its extended use, viz., the patent royalty, the cost of the engine, and the necessity of having a special form of railway.

No sooner had Blenkinsop shown that steam locomotion was practicable, than a rush of inventors followed in the same line, and a number of patents were immediately taken out for various forms of locomotive engines to suit the railways of the period. The Messrs. Chapman constructed an engine intended to pull itself along by means of a chain; William Hedley, the viewer of Mr. Blackett's colliery at Wylam, devised an engine to work on ordinary railways, the driving-wheels of which he proposed to arm with a double row of projecting teeth to bite into the ground, and thus give the engine a grip of the track; William Brunton, of Butterley Ironworks, Derbyshire, invented a locomotive, termed by him the "Mechanical Traveller," which was designed to push itself forward by means of legs, or levers, projecting behind.

The only one of these schemes that came to anything was Hedley's. By a series of experiments which he made Hedley found that he could obtain sufficient hauling power simply from the adhesion of the wheels of the locomotive to the rails, without any other accessory; and to him is due the merit of being the first to employ smooth-wheeled locomotives in the regular haulage of coal-waggons. His locomotive was known as the "Puffing Billy." It commenced working in 1813, and from this time locomotives continued to be employed in the haulage of the waggons on the Wylam railway.

Hedley's first engine had only one cylinder and a fly-wheel, and was rather unsteady in its working and difficult to manage; but it established the fact that locomotives with smooth wheels might be successfully employed on any railway approaching to a dead level. As at first constructed, however, its superiority to horses in point of economy was not very decided.

A circumstance more favourable to the introduction of steam locomotion in the North of England was the arrival of one of Blenkinsop's two-cylinder engines from Leeds, to work on the Kenton and Coxlodge Railway. The first trial of this engine took place on the 2nd of September, 1813. The event excited great interest and was witnessed by "a vast concourse of spectators." The engine was very highly approved of, and its complete success anticipated. It was designed to haul sixteen loaded waggons, of an aggregate weight of about seventy tons, at a speed of three and a half miles an hour.

About the same time another of Blenkinsop's locomotives was placed upon the railway at Orrell Colliery, Wigan; and from a letter of Blenkinsop's, dated 26th March, 1814, we learn that the engines at Leeds, Newcastle, and Wigan, were all "giving the greatest satisfaction," and were performing their work at one-sixth of the cost of horse-power.

Immediately after Blenkinsop's locomotive had been started on the Kenton and Coxlodge Railway, it was determined to adopt steam locomotion on the Killingworth Railway, which was situated in the immediate vicinity, and Mr. Stephenson accordingly set about the construction of an engine. Following the design of Blenkinsop's engine, he adopted a cylindrical wrought-iron boiler, with an internal wrought-iron fire-tube passing through it; two vertical cylinders of eight inches diameter and two-feet stroke, placed one in front of the other on the top of the boiler, and partially let into it; with cross-heads and connecting-rods to work the propelling gear. At this point, however, he deviated from Blenkinsop's plan, and avoiding the patent arrangement of pinion and rack-rail, he adopted smooth wheels, as Hedley had done. After being about ten months in making, the first trial of the engine took place on the 25th of July, 1814. Two days later it was tried on a piece of road, with edge-rails, ascending about 1 in 450. It dragged after it, exclusive of its own weight, eight loaded carriages, weighing altogether thirty tons, at the speed of four miles an hour, and after this time continued to work regularly.

Shortly afterwards Mr. Stephenson, in conjunction with another Killingworth engineer named Dodds, introduced a modification in another engine which was built, abandoning the spur-gearing and attaching the connecting-rods directly to the driving-wheels. This arrangement was patented by them in 1815. It was a simplification, but was not productive of unmixed good at the time. A chain was employed to couple the axles together, but great inconvenience arose from its liability to stretch in the course of working, which occasioned the driving-wheels to slip more or less at every stroke of the pistons, and caused a great loss of power. Mr. Wood estimated the loss from this source at about thirty per cent. of the power of the engine. This defect was obviated in Blenkinsop's engine, the spur-gearing and rack-rail being completely tied together by wheel-work, so that no slipping could take place—the object, indeed, for which the arrangement was invented.

For many years the smooth-wheeled locomotive made little headway; the weakness of the railways, and the immature character of the mechanism of the engine, being great drawbacks to its use. In 1816 a locomotive engine was purchased at Newcastle by Mr. Buddle, to work on the railways at Whitehaven Collieries, but its weight was found to be too much for the cast-iron rails, and after being tried for some time its use was discontinued. Another was procured from Mr. Stephenson in 1819, to work on the Duke of Portland's railway from Kilmarnock to Troon, in Scotland; but it, like the one above-mentioned, proved a failure, probably owing to the same cause.

The first railway on which locomotives were applied to any extent was the Hetton Colliery Railway. This important colliery, situated near the village of Hetton-le-Hole, in Durham, was commenced to be opened out in the year 1819, and required the construction of a line of railway to convey the coal to the shipping-places on the River Wear, some eight miles distant. Mr.

Stephenson, who still held the position of engineer to the Grand Allies, and resided at Killingworth, succeeded in obtaining the appointment of consulting engineer on the new line, his brother, Robert Stephenson, being resident engineer. The railway was commenced in 1819 and completed in 1822, and was constructed in accordance with Mr. Stephenson's ideas, and laid with a form of cast-iron rail designed and patented by himself and Mr. Losh, of Walker Ironworks, some years before. As the character of the country to be traversed precluded the construction of a level railway, it was necessary to employ various forms of hauling power. The line was opened for traffic on the 18th of November, 1822, the machinery employed to work it consisting of "five of Mr. George Stephenson's patent travelling engines, two sixty-horse power reciprocating engines, and five self-acting incline planes." The ill-success of the locomotives will be adverted to hereafter.

Though railways had been employed for conveying coal in the colliery districts for upwards of one hundred and fifty years, little or nothing had yet been done towards putting the invention to any other use. With two trifling exceptions the lines of railway were all in the hands of private companies; the exceptions being the small public railway constructed by Mr. Jessop at Loughborough, in Leicestershire, in 1789; and the railway from Merstham to Wandsworth, through Croydon, in Surrey, opened in 1803.

From the beginning of the present century the advocates for the employment of railways for purposes of ordinary traffic rapidly increased in number, and many lines were projected. At first it was proposed to connect large towns with each other by their means, but soon more comprehensive schemes were brought forward. One of the most earnest advocates for the general use of railways was Thomas Gray, a native of Leeds, who, in 1820, published a pamphlet entitled *Observations on a General Iron Railway, or Land Steam Conveyance, to supersede the necessity of Horses in all Public Vehicles,* &c. Gray proposed to employ Blenkinsop's locomotives to work the railway, and suggested the construction of "the first link" between the towns of Manchester and Liverpool.

Nothing came out of Gray's project for some years, but in the meantime a public company was formed to construct a railway between Stockton and Darlington, to open out the coal district of the south of Durham. This was a longer and more important line than any yet made. An Act of Parliament was obtained in 1823; and Mr. Stephenson, having obtained the appointment of engineer, left Killingworth to superintend its construction.

We have seen that in some instances light malleable-iron rails had been already employed on the top of wooden ones with satisfactory results, but previous to 1820 they were only used very sparingly and in short lengths of two or three feet. In this year the use of rails of malleable iron received a great impulse from the invention of the process of *rolling* them in lengths of about eighteen feet. The process was invented and patented by Mr. Birkenshaw, of Bedlington Ironworks, Northumberland; and from this period the use of rails of cast iron began to decline, and malleable-iron rails to take their place. These, however, were still made of a light section, weighing at most about 28 lbs. per yard.

The great superiority of the new material led Mr. Stephenson to recommend the adoption of malleable-iron rails on the Stockton and Darlington Railway, but on account of their extra cost it was decided to lay only one-half of the line with malleable-iron and the other half with cast-iron rails.

The country through which the railway passed admitted of the construction of a more level line than that at Hetton Colliery, it being necessary to employ only one fixed engine, while the remainder of the road admitted of being worked either by means of locomotive engines or horses. It was accordingly decided to apply both to the work of haulage. The line was opened for traffic on the 27th of September, 1825; and one locomotive was added after another till four were in use, three of which were supplied by Mr. Stephenson, and the fourth by Mr. Robert Wilson of Newcastle, while the surplus traffic was carried on by means of horses.

Even at this time the superiority of the smooth-wheeled locomotive engine to fixed engines and horses was by no means decided. At Hetton Colliery three of the locomotives had actually been abandoned after some years' trial, and fixed engines substituted; and in 1827 it was a matter of consideration whether the two remaining locomotives should not likewise be taken off the line, and their places also be filled by reciprocating engines. Neither on the Stockton and Darlington Railway do the locomotives appear to have given any measure of satisfaction; indeed the idea of their abandonment, in favour of horses, is stated to have been seriously entertained in 1827.

For a considerable number of years no improvement, of any importance, had been effected in the locomotive. Its rate of speed was ordinarily about four or five miles an hour, and its load about thirty or forty tons in summer, and much less in winter. The first individual to introduce a number of novel and highly successful alterations in its mechanism was Timothy Hackworth, an ingenious mechanic who had had considerable experience in the building of locomotives. Hackworth was a native of Wylam, and had aided in the construction of the locomotives there; for a short period he acted as superintendent of the engine factory established at Newcastle-on-Tyne by Mr. Stephenson and Mr. Pease; and after the opening of the Stockton and Darlington Railway he was appointed manager of the working department on the new line. He was well acquainted with the weak points of the locomotives then in use, and was impressed with the conviction that they were susceptible of great improvement. Having obtained the sanction of the railway directors, he set about constructing an engine, after his own design, in 1827. Departing from the usual plan of having the cylinders connected to different shafts, he placed them on opposite sides of the boiler, and applied the connecting rods to the same axle-tree; at the same time he adopted the return fire-tube, which was used by Trevithick and Hedley, in lieu of the straight flue employed in Blenkinsop's and Stephenson's engines; and by contracting the orifice through which the exhaust steam entered the chimney, he greatly increased the force of the steam blast and effected a more vigorous combustion in the furnace, thus obtaining a greater command of steam. The locomotive in which the above improved arrangements were first combined was named the "Royal George," and was the most efficient and powerful engine which had yet been built. Hackworth's improvements introduced a new type of locomotive, and aided to a considerable extent in the establishment of the locomotive system. From this time Blenkinsop's and George Stephenson's engines went out of date, and in all the new locomotives the cylinders were placed at the sides of the boiler, and applied to drive the same axle.

The locomotive engine and the railway system, however, were not established upon a firm foundation until after the construction of the Liverpool and Manchester Railway, of which also Mr. Stephenson was engineer. On this line malleable-iron rails alone were used, though those first laid down were of a very light section. Even at the date of the completion of this line much difficulty was experienced in deciding upon the hauling power to be adopted; but as it was evident that horse-power was inadequate to cope with the expected traffic, the choice lay between locomotives and fixed engines.

The events which brought about a decision in favour of locomotives are well known. By the happy combination of the multitubular boiler and the steam-blast, Mr. Robert Stephenson succeeded in producing, in the "Rocket," an engine far superior to any previously built, both in point of speed and efficiency. The necessity for adopting a heavier form of rail, and heavier engines, was at once apparent. The railway was relaid with heavy rails at considerable cost; heavier locomotives were built; and from this time the superiority of the railway system to every other mode of conveyance was placed beyond question. The building of railways commenced in earnest soon afterwards in nearly every part of the country; and the two Stephensons, father and son, rose rapidly to fame and fortune as the first railway engineers in the kingdom.

Another use of the steam-engine, which dates from the beginning of the present century, and which gave a powerful impulse to the trade of the country, and particularly to the coal trade, was its application to propelling boats. From the time of the invention of the double-acting engine by Watt, the solution of the problems of steam locomotion and steam navigation advanced *pari passu*; and it is a singular coincidence that in the same year and the same month that the first locomotive engine commenced to work regularly at Leeds, the first successful steam-boat in Europe was launched by Henry Bell on the Clyde, the date of both events being June, 1812. Within a few years from this time the application of steam-boats to tow vessels into and out of harbours put an end to the custom, hitherto pursued, of closing the northern collieries for two months during the winter season.

In addition to the direct and indirect advantages accruing to the coal trade from the extended use of the steam-engine, other circumstances conspired at this time to impart a powerful stimulus to the trade. The increased demand for iron, for railways and other purposes, gave a great impulse to the iron manufacture, which again reacted on the coal trade. Besides, a new and important demand for coal sprang up at this period from another source. In the first era of its history the mineral had been employed only as a source of heat; after the invention of the steam-engine it had become available as a source of power; now a commencement was made to utilise it as a source of light. The idea of lighting towns by means of coal gas, conveyed from a central point through iron pipes, was at first ridiculed by many as an impossibility. One member of a Parliamentary Committee is stated to have experienced much difficulty in grasping the idea of "a light without a wick." But it was soon ascertained that the project was neither impossible nor impracticable, and town after town became rapidly supplied with its establishment of gas-works, gas-pipes, and gas-lamps; and the means of obtaining a cheap, brilliant, and easily managed light, were placed at the command of every householder.

Thus it happened that, from various causes, the coal trade entered upon a period of greater activity than ever at the beginning of the present century. According to the most reliable estimates, the total production of coal in the country in 1800 was about ten millions of tons per annum. In 1830 it was estimated to have risen to twenty millions of tons: the metropolis alone consuming two millions of tons, in the conveyance of which from the northern collieries a fleet of fourteen hundred boats was employed.

The opening up of the interior of the country, which had been partially effected by means of canals during the latter part of the eighteenth century, went on with much greater rapidity after the general introduction of railways began. Great facilities for the transport of coal were thus presented to all the mining districts, and the way paved for the prodigious development of the coal and iron industries which has since taken place.

CHAPTER XVIII.

DEEPER AND MORE DIFFICULT WINNINGS.

"The results deducible from Smith's discovery afford another pregnant example of the economic application of purely theoretical principles, which in their first conception seemed but little connected with the furtherance of our material prosperity."—
PROF. A. C. RAMSAY.

IN the south-eastern portion of the county of Durham the coal-measures are overlapped and concealed by a more recent and unconformable formation belonging to the Permian system, and known as the Magnesian Limestone. The depth at which the coal lay, added to the unpromising character of the surface, had hitherto presented an effectual barrier to the development of this part of the coal-field. Coal had been worked at Ferryhill, under the covering of limestone, in the latter part of the eighteenth century, but the seam appears to have been of inferior quality; and it had become the universal opinion of the mining engineers of the north that the coal deteriorated when it passed under the limestone rock—a belief which had taken the form of the dictum "No coal under the Magnesian Limestone."

In remarkable contrast to this were the views of Dr. William Smith, who for many years had been industriously engaged in mapping out the surface rocks in various parts of the kingdom, and tracing their relative positions—in fact working out the great idea he had conceived that the rocky strata preserved an unvarying order like the leaves of a book; and that though some were occasionally wanting, none were ever found out of their true place in the series. This was only rendered possible by means of the important discovery he had made that each rock formation contained organic remains peculiar to the era in which it had been deposited, which gave an infallible clue to the identification of the strata belonging to it wherever found. Smith was thus laying the foundation of the modern science of geology.

In the course of his practice as an engineer and mineral surveyor, Smith accidentally met with Colonel Braddyll, in London, which led to his being employed by that gentleman, in 1821-2, to make a survey of some estates belonging to him in Lancashire, Cumberland, and Durham. The interest which Smith felt in the properties in the two former counties was altogether inferior to that with which he scrutinised the estate in Durham. This included the village of Haswell, and comprised seven hundred acres of poor land, situated on the Magnesian Limestone, and regarded as of little value by Colonel Braddyll's agents. The proprietors of adjoining estates shared the same opinion, few of them believing that their properties had any other than surface value. Smith, however, at once saw that the limestone was an unconformable cover to the coal-measures; and having traced the course of these, and estimated the thickness of the limestone, he inferred that the best seams of coal would be found at an attainable depth at Haswell.

No immediate steps were taken to open out the coal in Colonel Braddyll's property, but within a few years sinkings through the limestone were effected elsewhere, and the correctness of Smith's inductions abundantly verified; and this extensive area, hitherto regarded as of no value, became the scene of the winning of some of the largest, deepest, and most costly collieries that had yet been opened out.

The work of piercing through the limestone, to the coal-measures beneath, was in some cases attended with extraordinary difficulty and cost. This was partly occasioned by the open character of the rock itself, which, being intersected by numerous large fissures, discharged vast quantities of water into the shafts; but a still more formidable difficulty presented itself in most cases when the bottom of the limestone was reached. Here, at the break between the two unconformable formations, a bed of loose sand existed, of varying consistency and thickness, but always yielding great feeders of water, to penetrate through which was at times a task of immensely greater difficulty than cutting the hardest rock.

Foremost among the deep sinkings made through the Magnesian Limestone, alike in point of time, depth, and boldness of conception, was the famous pit put down by the Messrs. Pemberton at Monkwearmouth. Sinking was commenced in May, 1826, and notwithstanding great difficulty and discouragement, the works were pushed forward in a spirited and determined manner. The progress, however, was slow, and it was not till August, 1831, that the first unequivocal stratum of the coal formation was reached. This consisted of a seam of coal one and a half inches in thickness, found at the depth of 344 feet from the surface. The thickness of the covering of limestone was 325 feet, and the stratum of sand, at the breach between the Permian formation and the coal-measures, was five feet thick. At the bottom of the limestone the feeders of water amounted to 3,000 gallons per minute, but this was soon dammed back by a casing of cast-iron tubbing, which was carried from the little seam of coal above mentioned to within seventy-eight feet from the surface.

For a considerable distance into the coal-measures the undertaking appeared very unpromising, as a greater thickness of barren strata was pierced than had ever been encountered previously. A new feeder of water was met with at the depth of 1,000 feet, requiring fresh pumps and a fresh outlay of money. In the eyes of most men the prospects of the enterprising adventurers seemed dark indeed; by many of the coal-owners the project was denounced as hopeless. But the Messrs. Pemberton boldly persevered, sinking deeper and deeper, until in February, 1834, their pluck was rewarded by the shaft reaching a seam of coal of considerable thickness and value at the depth of 267 fathoms from the surface. This seam was found to be identical with the Bensham seam of the Tyne, or Maudlin seam of the Wear, and the shaft was afterwards carried down further to the still more valuable Hutton seam, which was sunk to in April, 1846, at a depth of 287 fathoms, or 1,720 feet from the surface. The winning of this colliery is stated to have cost about 100,000*l.*

In the meantime a number of other sinkings had been carried down through the limestone. The first attempt made at Haswell, by the Haswell Coal Company, was abandoned, after an expenditure of 60,000*l.*, on account of the stratum of quicksand encountered by the shaft, at the bottom of the limestone, proving twenty fathoms thick. The second attempt was more fortunate. By means of boring, a spot was found free from quicksand, and here a shaft was sunk which reached the Hutton seam in March, 1835, after five years' labour, at a depth of 155 fathoms.

Coincidently with the above sinking another was made in the northern part of the same township by Colonel Braddyll and partners (the South Hetton Coal Company), which, after piercing fifty-seven fathoms of limestone and five fathoms of sand, reached the Hutton seam, at a depth of 180 fathoms, in 1833.

A few years later the same company, being desirous to increase their powers of producing coal, commenced to open out another colliery, at Murton, which proved one of the most difficult and costly winnings ever effected. In the beginning of 1838 two pits, each fourteen feet in diameter, were begun, and carried forward simultaneously, at a spot where it had been ascertained by boring that the limestone was seventy-six fathoms thick, and the sand below from five to six fathoms. The feeders of water encountered in piercing the limestone were successively tubbed off, so that immediately previous to the bed of sand being reached the shafts were free from water. On the 26th of June, 1839, when one of the shafts approached the top of the quicksand, the sand-feeders burst upwards through four feet of strong limestone which intervened; and before the pumps could be heaved up they were all choked, and ten feet of sand deposited in the bottom of the pit.

It having been found that the engine power at this

shaft was unable to make any impression upon the water, several large bore-holes were made through the bottom of the other shaft, then close upon the sand, in order that the united engine power of both pits might be applied. By this means water was drawn at the rate of 4,678 gallons per minute, but no sensible impression was made on the feeders, so that the further progress of the sinking was effectually prevented.

Nothing daunted by the extraordinary difficulties which had presented themselves, the indomitable adventurers determined to redouble their efforts. A third shaft, 16 feet in diameter (being larger than any hitherto sunk), was commenced, and fitted with an unprecedented force of engine power—two pumping engines, and two winding engines, adapted also to pump, being erected upon it. The new pit was pushed forward with all expedition, and in six months was completed to the depth of 73 fathoms.

The total engine power now available, in the three shafts, consisted of three pumping engines, and six winding engines; working twenty-seven columns of pumps; and supplied with steam from thirty-nine boilers.

When all preparations had been made, the sinking of all three shafts through the sand was commenced simultaneously. The engines drew 10,000 gallons of water per minute. The scouring action of the sand and water on the buckets and working-barrels greatly impeded the work; the buckets being frequently worn out at the end of two or three hours. For some time the cost of the leather required for buckets amounted to 11*l*. 5*s*. per hour—three tan-yards being kept in operation to supply it. At length, however, the energy of the adventurers was rewarded by all the shafts being successfully carried down through the sand, and the whole of the water effectually stopped back by cast-iron tubbing. The two original pits were then continued downwards, and on the 15th of April, 1843, the Hutton seam was reached at the depth of 248 fathoms. The cost of this sinking is stated to have been from 250,000*l*. to 300,000*l*.; of which 30,000*l*. was due to the expense incurred in piercing the quicksand. The large shaft, however, afterwards proved invaluable for purposes of ventilation.

A number of other sinkings were carried down through the Magnesian Limestone about the same time; Shotton Colliery was won in 1841; Castle Eden Colliery in 1842; Trimdon Colliery in 1843; followed by other important winnings at Seaham, Ryhope, &c.; but in none of these cases were the difficulties encountered so formidable as in the sinking at Murton.

CHAPTER XIX.

INVENTION OF CAGES, AND IRON-WIRE ROPES.

FOR a long period after the use of double waterwheels, in raising the coal out of the pits, was superseded by the direct application of the steam-engine—in other respects the machinery employed in this work had undergone little or no alteration in the North of England collieries—the coal continued to be drawn to the day in the ancient corf, or basket, made of hazel rods; and the ropes or cables employed, whether round or flat, were invariably made of hemp.

As the pits increased in depth, the size of the corves had been enlarged until they commonly carried five or six cwts. of coal; and iron "bows" had been substituted for wooden ones. It many cases too it had become customary to draw two or three corves at a time, attached to the rope one above the other at short distances apart. But they were still swung loosely up and down the shafts, and suffered great damage from striking against each other, or against the sides of the pit, in ascending and descending. At times these collisions resulted in the empty corf being carried back again to the surface, perched on the top of the ascending full one. The only improvement in the drawing of the corves consisted in dividing the shaft by a timber brattice throughout its whole length, thus providing separate passages for the ascending and descending loads. This effectually put a stop to direct collisions, but did not alleviate the damage sustained against the sides of the pit.

The use of corves was attended with many other inconveniences. Being high, they were difficult to fill at the hewer's working place. At the junction between the branch railways and the horse roads they required to be lifted from the small trams on to the horse rolley by means of a crane. They were unwieldy to handle, both at the top and bottom of the shaft; they required endless repairs; while the largest quantity of coal that could be drawn by an engine, in twelve hours winding did not exceed 300 tons.

Under the corf system, the arrangements for lowering and raising the men and boys were of the most unsafe and primitive description. Their security depended entirely on the tenacity with which they clung to the rope. The general practice, in ascending and descending, was for two men to sit each with a leg in a loop of the chain; and frequently five or six boys would cling to the rope, one above another, trusting their lives to their capability of holding fast while the rope traversed a distance of 1,600, or even 1,800 feet. So inured were the boys to this hazardous mode of travelling, that it was regarded by them as "fine fun." Mr. Buddle relates an instance of a little fellow, who, in descending a pit 100 fathoms deep, fell fast asleep on the way, with his arms clasped round the rope, and in this condition was brought back to the top again, when he was pulled off by the banksman, and even then was only awakened by a slap.

Though the ingenious arrangements introduced by Mr. Curr at Sheffield, in the latter part of the eighteenth century, for raising the coal in carriages, were found to answer very well in shallow collieries, they were not sufficiently matured to admit of their application in deep ones. The carriage being suspended at the end of the rope, it was scarcely possible to raise more than one at a time; and the mechanism for landing the load at the surface was somewhat clumsy and tedious.

An improved arrangement had come into use at some of the collieries in the south, where the carriage, instead of being suspended, was drawn sitting on a platform. It appears to have been introduced in connection with the balance-tub system of winding—the carriage sitting on the top of the water cistern. The arrangement was simple and efficient, admitting of 300 or 400 tons being drawn in a day, from a depth of fifty or sixty fathoms. Its use, however, appears to have been limited to raising one carriage at a time, under the peculiar circumstances above mentioned.

Matters were in this state when the subject of improvements in winding arrangements was taken up by Mr. T. Y. Hall, and a series of experiments commenced with a view to the disuse of corves, which resulted in the abolition of the ancient system and the invention of a new and immensely superior one. Mr. Hall was a native of Greenside, near Ryton. In his early youth he went through an unusual amount of drudgery as a common pit boy. Subsequently he served an apprenticeship under his father and Mr. Buddle, at Towneley, Whitefield, and Crawcrook Collieries. From thence he removed in 1826 to take the management of North Hetton Colliery; and after holding this position for a period of four years he was appointed manager of South Hetton and Blackboy Collieries.

It was at South Hetton Colliery, the sinking of which to a depth of 180 fathoms was completed, as we have seen, in 1833, that Mr. Hall first attempted to employ substitutes for the wicker-work corves. His earliest experiment, made in the summer of this year, consisted in fitting up one of the shafts with large iron tubs capable of carrying $1\frac{1}{2}$ tons of coal each. To steady the tubs, and prevent them suffering or causing damage by oscillation, the compartments in which they travelled were cleaded round with timber, thus presenting a smooth passage only slightly larger than the size of the tub. In the underground workings small wheel carriages were employed to convey the coal between the working places and the pit bottom, where the contents of four carriages were emptied into a tub and so drawn to the surface.

This arrangement, however, was open to a number of serious objections, and after it had undergone about six months' trial, and its superiority to corves was doubtful, the owners of the colliery employed Messrs. Nicholas Wood and George Johnson to report upon the system. These gentlemen accordingly visited the colliery early in 1834, and inspected Mr. Hall's new arrangements, but with the result of being led to report unfavourably of them. Several drawbacks were urged against the system, viz., the difficulty of properly screening the contents of the large tubs; the impossibility of discriminating between the colliers who sent clean and those who sent dirty coal; and the breakage of coal attendant upon the emptying of the carriages into the tubs at the pit bottom.

Mr. Hall being dissatisfied with the condemnation of his system requested two other engineers to examine into the matter, who in their report, dated April 10th, 1834, recommended that a further trial should be given to it. The owners of the colliery accordingly did not interfere; but soon afterwards Mr. Hall, in pondering over the objections urged against the system by Messrs. Wood and Johnson, succeeded in devising another plan, whereby they were entirely obviated. This was to substitute a *cage*, or chair, for the iron tub, in which to draw the carriages themselves to the surface with their contents.

No time was lost by Mr. Hall in making trial of his new scheme. Another shaft was prepared for the reception of cages. Passages for them to travel in were closely cleaded with timber, in a manner similar to that employed in guiding the large iron tubs. The bottoms of the cages were provided with short pieces of rail, which constituted a connecting link between the railways underground and those on the surface, and afforded great facility for running the carriages on and off the cages at the top and bottom of the shaft.

The cage system was brought into operation in December, 1834, but shortly afterwards Mr. Hall left South Hetton Colliery to undertake the management of collieries in the vicinity of Ryton, which he had leased conjointly with Messrs. Buddle and Potter, and for some reason the new system was temporarily discontinued after his departure. But Mr. Hall, being convinced of the great value of the invention, at once proceeded to apply it in a more mature form at the Glebe pit, Woodside, near Ryton. Here, *shoes* and *guide-rods* were adopted, in lieu of the cleaded passages previously employed; *keps* also were applied to rest the cages upon during the process of changing the carriages; and the immense superiority of the new system was quickly felt, from the circumstance that the pit was able to draw twice as much coal as was possible under the old arrangement.

A beautiful model of a pit-shaft, fitted up on the cage and guide system, was made in the year 1835 by the late Mr. Thomas Sopwith, F.R.S., which, after being exhibited at the Polytechnic Exhibition at Newcastle, was presented in 1853 to the Museum of Practical Geology, London.

The value of Mr. Hall's system was soon recognised. Numbers of persons visited the Glebe pit to see it in operation; and the success which attended it led to its speedy adoption at one colliery after another. From this time the use of the ancient corves rapidly declined, and the employment of cages and carriages soon became general.

The change was productive of many highly important advantages. Leaving out of view the economy effected by it, it need only be mentioned that the men and boys could be lowered and raised with immensely greater comfort and safety; while the rapidity with which the winding could be carried on enabled the output of the collieries to be more than doubled.

In addition to the introduction of the cage and

guide system, Mr. Hall also effected a great improvement in the underground roads, by substituting light malleable-iron edge-rails and flange-wheels for the cast-iron tram-plates and sharp wheels previously employed between the horse roads and the working faces. Thus he completed the improvements which Mr. Curr had begun, and established the system of drawing and conveying coal in carriages as now universally practised.

A curious result of the disuse of corves in the northern collieries was that it had the effect of permanently lowering the price of nuts in the London market.

The era which witnessed the substitution of cages and carriages for the ancient corves, also witnessed the substitution of ropes of iron-wire for the hemp ropes previously employed. The new ropes were first applied to mining purposes in the Hartz mountains, and were the invention of Mr. Albert, principal officer of the mining administration at Clausthal. The economy of the iron-wire ropes, added to their lightness and durability, soon led to their extensive use. In 1835–6 they found their way into collieries in Prussia, and immediately afterwards they were introduced into the collieries of the North of England. Here they were first applied in raising the coal in a staple, or underground pit, at St. Lawrence Colliery, near Newcastle. An account of these ropes was given by Count Breuner, of Hungary, a chief director of mines, in a paper communicated to the British Association at the meeting held at Newcastle in 1838. The subject, it is stated, did not appear to attract the attention it deserved at the time, but within a few years afterwards iron-wire ropes had been introduced in various parts of the Great Northern coal-field, both in working inclines and in raising the coal in the shafts; being usually round in the former and flat in the latter case. Much opposition was made by the pitmen to the adoption of the new ropes for winding, and the dispute ultimately assumed the form of an assize trial at Durham, in July, 1844. This important trial—known as the Wingate Colliery Wire Rope Trial—decided the question, the evidence adduced fully demonstrating the superiority of the wire ropes to those made of hemp, and from this time the use of the latter rapidly declined.

CHAPTER XX.

INTERVENTION OF THE LEGISLATURE IN MINING OPERATIONS.

For about twenty years after the Sunderland Society had ceased to exist, the subject of accidents in mines received little attention from the general public, and yet perhaps at no time were the collieries in a more unsatisfactory state. Notwithstanding the invention of the safety-lamp, the number of lives lost in the mines had become greater instead of less.

This arose from a variety of circumstances. The quantity of coal raised, and number of persons employed in the mines, had greatly increased. In all parts of the country the mines were becoming deeper and more fiery. Seams of coal which had previously lain unwrought, on account of their fiery character, had been opened out, and were now being worked by the aid of the safety-lamp. Large numbers of mines also continued to be worked, at considerable risk, with naked lights, either because the miners objected to use the safety-lamp on account of the diminished light which it gave, or because its use was considered to be incompatible with the employment of gunpowder in getting the coal.

The fact that the efforts of private individuals to compass the safe and efficient working of coal and other mines required to be supplemented by aids of a more comprehensive character, had on several occasions been brought into public notice. As early as 1797 a far-seeing scheme had been suggested by Mr. Thomas, of Denton, for establishing an office at Newcastle-on-Tyne for the collection and registration of plans and sections of the various collieries in the district, one of the principal objects in view being the prevention of accidents in the future from coal workings unexpectedly encountering unknown and unsuspected excavations filled with water or noxious gases. The subject was revived by Mr. W. Chapman, in 1815, after the great inundation at Heaton Colliery, when seventy-five lives were lost, as already mentioned, by the bursting in of water from some old workings, no plan of which existed—a catastrophe which occurred notwithstanding that great precautions were taken to prevent it by a careful system of boring. The scheme suggested by Mr. Thomas only contemplated a voluntary registration of records in the Newcastle-on-Tyne district, but Mr. Chapman's proposal went much further, recommending that such a movement should be initiated in all the coal-mining districts, and setting forth that the preservation of plans of abandoned or exhausted workings was a matter worthy of the attention of the Legislature, and should be made compulsory by Act of Parliament.

The above schemes were both brought forward in papers read before the Literary and Philosophical Society of Newcastle-on-Tyne, and, with a liberality and public spirit deserving of all praise, this society published both papers at its own expense in 1813, but the movement failed to elicit any response at the time.

The frequency with which explosions, and other accidents, continued to take place in the mines, at last had the effect of forcing the matter under the notice of Parliament; and on the motion of Mr. Pease, member for South Durham, a Select Committee of the House of Commons was appointed on the 2nd of June, 1835, "to inquire into the nature, cause, and extent of those lamentable catastrophes which have occurred in the mines of Great Britain, with the view of ascertaining and suggesting the means for preventing the recurrence of similar fatal accidents." The necessity for the step which had been taken was forcibly exemplified immediately afterwards by the occurrence of an explosion more disastrous than any that had yet taken place. This happened at Wallsend Colliery on the 18th of June, and occasioned the loss of 102 lives.

The committee commenced its labours on the 17th of June, and continued to hold investigations till the 30th of July. Many witnesses were examined, consisting of mining engineers from all the principal mining districts, scientific gentlemen, &c. It was before this committee that the security afforded by the Davy lamp was first publicly impugned, and one or two instances were adduced in which the lamp appeared to have given rise to explosion. Sir Humphry Davy himself, however, was well aware that under certain contingencies explosion might be communicated through the wire gauze, and warned the miners against exposing the lamp, in an unprotected condition, to a strong current of gas or explosive mixture.

An interesting account of an experiment made expressly to illustrate this source of danger was given by Mr. Buddle to the committee. It took place at one of the Earl of Durham's collieries, shortly after the invention of the lamp. The experiment was made in the presence of Sir H. Davy and a number of gentlemen. At this colliery the gas issuing from a strong blower in the shaft had been conveyed to the surface, where it discharged itself through a cast-iron pipe.

"We took a length of hose from an extinguishing engine," says Mr. Buddle, "with the jet-pipe upon it, and attached that to the blower-pipe at the top of the pit; it was held horizontally and the jet was thrown very forcibly out of the nozzle of the pipe; the blower was sufficiently strong to propel the stream of gas across the engine-house. I well recollect the pipe was held at the entrance of the engine-house, and the jet passed the explosion nearly to the far end of the room, for it was very powerful; the distance that the blower fired it was from nine to twelve feet, I should think. I held the lamp in the direction of the jet, and not having seen it before, I was not very apprehensive of its firing. It did not fire at first, but as I approached the end of the nozzle-pipe, the gauze became heated red-hot, and passed the explosion. The flame was as long, or longer, than the breadth of the engine-room; I remember that it burnt the nap off my great coat and spoilt it. This experiment was repeated over and over again. Lord Durham himself was present, and a great many other persons, professional men and others, were present on this occasion. The force of Sir Humphry's remarks at the time was—'Now, gentlemen, you see the nature of the danger to which you are exposed in using the lamp, and I caution you to guard against it in the manner I have shown you. This is to show the only case in which the lamp will explode, and I caution and warn you not to use it in any such case when you can avoid it, without using the shield.'"

The experience of Mr. Buddle was in direct opposition to the allegations of those who cavilled at the value of the Davy lamp. He informed the committee that during the twenty years that had intervened since the invention of the lamp, there had been from 1,000 to 1,500 lamps in daily use in the collieries under his care, and he never knew an explosion to happen from it—"not even one solitary instance." At this time the collieries superintended by Mr. Buddle were amongst the most fiery in the kingdom; but the safety-lamps were tended with great care, and, in accordance with Sir H. Davy's instructions, were cautiously sheltered when being carried in dangerous currents. The necessity for protecting the lamp in this way, however, was not universally known, some mining engineers now learning of it for the first time.

Among the more novel suggestions made to the committee may be mentioned Mr. Goldsworthy Gurney's proposal to exclude fire altogether from the mines—to effect the lighting of the workings by means of reflected light, and the ventilation by means of jets of high-pressure steam; and that of John Martin, the artist, to substitute a large exhausting fan, driven by a steam-engine, in lieu of the ventilating furnace.

After having taken a large amount of evidence, besides having witnessed a series of experiments with many varieties of safety-lamps in the laboratory of London University, the committee drew up a report, which they presented on the 4th of September. They regretted, they said, that the results of their inquiry had not enabled them to propound any particular plan whereby mining accidents might be avoided with certainty. They expressed their conviction that some mines required more shafts than were ordinarily provided; that the use of bratticed shafts was deservedly reprobated; that the foul and free air-courses were frequently too near to each other, the communications not adequately protected, and the length of the air-courses excessive; that in some mines lighted with naked lights the use of the safety-lamp ought to be compelled by the owners; that it was essential to have correct maps and plans, &c. They suggested that notice of accidents attended with great loss of life should be transmitted to the Secretary of State for the Home Department, and that some fit and proper person or persons should be appointed on such occasions to attend the inquest and assist the coroner and jury in their investigations.

They had also seriously considered how far legislative enactments might promote the safety of the miners, but regarded it as impossible then to lay down any precise directions, or to frame any rules of universal application. They thought, however, that great benefit might be anticipated from men of known ability being encouraged to visit the mines, whether in the character of distinguished chemists, mechanists, or philanthropists; that great advantages might be obtained from the establishment of associations in the mining districts similar to the Polytechnic School recently formed in Cornwall; and that the employment of properly qualified persons, supported by a sufficient number of subordinate overseers, together with the observance of strict discipline in the mines, might be the means of preventing many accidents.

The labours of the Select Committee of 1835 resulted in the collection of much interesting and valuable information regarding the subject of their inquiry, which, together with their comments based upon it, was laid before the House of Commons and the country; but they did not suggest the adoption of any measures to give force to their recommendations, and nothing further was done in the matter, so that the inquiry, for the time being, proved practically abortive.

The dangerous condition of the mines, however, continued to force itself into public notice by means of the explosions which occurred from time to time, and in consequence of a heavy explosion which happened in the St. Hilda pit at South Shields in June, 1839, by which fifty-two lives were lost, at the suggestion of Mr. James Mather, made at a public meeting called together to consider the matter, a number of gentlemen immediately formed themselves into a committee to investigate the causes of mine accidents.

This committee—known as the South Shields Committee—carried on investigations for a period of three years, taking great pains to acquaint themselves with the subject in a variety of ways, viz. by visiting and making experiments in the mines; by the examination of good practical pitmen; by communication with some of the ablest viewers of the country; by correspondence with distinguished scientific men; and by investigation of the mining laws and regulations of foreign states.

In 1843 they published their report, a most able

and valuable document, the views promulgated in which were in many respects far in advance of the standard of the time. Their opinions, if somewhat pronounced, were on the whole remarkably correct, sound, sagacious, and practical.

With regard to safety-lamps, they came to the conclusion that no mere safety-lamp is able to secure fiery mines from explosion, and that to rely upon the safety-lamp is a fatal error; that the naked Davy lamp, without a complete shield, is a most dangerous instrument; and that the best form of safety-lamp is of the Clanny or Mueseler description, in which the supply of air is derived entirely from the upper part of the construction, over the glass shield.

But that, whether from overmuch reliance on safety-lamps, or other cause, the far more important and safer system of ventilation had been comparatively neglected, and the condition of the ventilation of the fiery mines of the north was of the most dangerous description, caused by too few shafts in proportion to the extent of underground workings, the only remedy for which was more shafts and more air. No new mine they said, should be allowed to be worked unless two distinct and separate shafts had previously been put down, which should be secured by Act of Parliament.

They were very favourably impressed with the system of ventilating mines by jets of high-pressure steam, as proposed by Mr. Goldsworthy Gurney, and strongly recommended its adoption. They also urged the employment of the system of draining off gas by means of drifts specially made for the purpose, as introduced by Ryan. They suggested that all collieries should be provided with scientific instruments for ascertaining atmospheric changes and the velocity of the air-current.

The necessity for the registration of plans and sections of mines they considered sufficiently obvious, and submitted, that from the well-digested arrangements of foreign states some useful suggestions might be obtained in organising a good system in this country.

They considered that as a rule the education of the chief officers of mines, in respect to scientific attainments, was far inferior to the high responsibility of their office, and that as the Legislature already required a systematic professional education in the case of the learned professions, as well as in the army and navy, the same principle should be extended to the mining profession, which is so important to the best interests of the country, and involves the lives of so many of her people.

They likewise urged the necessity for the establishment of a system of Government inspection of mines, on the principle already acknowledged and acted upon by the Legislature with regard to railways, &c., and applied in the mines on the Continent with great advantage.

The subject of infant labour in the mines did not

escape the attention of the South Shields Committee; but while they had been engaged upon their investigation into the causes of accidents, a Royal Commission—the Children's Employment Commission—had been conducting an inquiry into the state of the mining population with special reference to the employment of young persons in the mines. The information elicited revealed the existence of a state of matters which had been little suspected. Soon after the publication of the report of the Royal Commissioners, Lord Ashley (afterwards Lord Shaftesbury) introduced a measure prohibiting the employment of women and girls underground, and restricting the employment of boys. The measure received the royal assent on the 10th of August, 1842, and came into full operation on the 1st of March, 1843, after which date it became illegal to employ any female whatever underground, or any boys under the age of ten years, except such as were already in the pits at the time. This Act did not contemplate subterranean inspection of mines, (indeed Lord Ashley himself regarded this as altogether impossible at that time,) but it provided for the appointment of inspectors to visit mines and collieries to see that the provisions of the Act were observed. In November, 1843, Mr. Seymour Tremenheere was appointed inspector, and his reports were presented annually to both Houses of Parliament until the office was abolished some sixteen years afterwards.

From this time mines continued to receive a large amount of attention from the Government, and all the more serious accidents which occurred were made the subject of a special investigation.

In 1844 a great explosion took place at Haswell Colliery, Durham, by which ninety-five lives were lost. In consequence of a petition from the miners, praying for the appointment of a Commission to inquire into the circumstances, Professors Lyell and Faraday were instructed by the Government to attend the inquest, examine the mine, and draw up a report of the results of their investigations. The visit of these two scientific gentlemen, however, did not prove a success; though it must be admitted that they undertook the task with reluctance, and advanced their recommendations with great modesty, and with due deference to the opinions of persons more practically conversant with the subject. They confined their attention almost entirely to the ventilation of the goaves, or wastes, which they proposed to effect by carrying off the gas into the upcast shaft, or return air-way, through ranges of cast-iron pipes twelve inches in diameter. Their views provoked much adverse criticism, and the plan proposed was condemned by a Committee of the Coal Trade, on account of its impracticability, its cost, and its inefficacy to prevent explosions. It was shown that, exclusively of the Haswell accident, eleven great explosions had occurred in the Northumberland and Durham collieries during the preceding fourteen years, and that these, with only one exception of a doubtful character, had all happened in parts of the mines where pillar-working had not commenced, or, in other words, where goaves did not exist.

Sir Charles Lyell relates an amusing incident which happened during the visit to Haswell. In the course of one of their underground examinations, Faraday asked the overmen how they ascertained the velocity of the air-current travelling through the mine. They said they would show him, which they proceeded to do by igniting a small quantity of loose gunpowder, and observing the time taken by the smoke to pass a given distance. Faraday expressed himself satisfied, but, being surprised at the seemingly careless way in which they handled the gunpowder, he asked where they kept their stock of that material. They told him they kept it in a bag, the neck of which was tied up tight. "But where," said Faraday, "do you keep the bag?" "You are sitting on it," was the reply; they having given this soft and yielding seat, as the most comfortable one at hand, to the commissioner. Faraday instantly sprang to his feet, and in the most animated and impressive style expostulated with them for their carelessness, which he said was especially discreditable to those who should be setting an example of vigilance and caution to others.

From the time that the necessity for a Government

jurisdiction of the mines of this country, similar to that exercised over mines on the Continent, had been urgently recommended by the South Shields Committee, the number of advocates for the intervention of the Legislature, and the appointment of Government inspectors of mines, continued to increase. Prominent among these was Mr. Matthias Dunn, who, in his *View of the Coal Trade of the North of England,* published in 1844, and in his *Review of the Report of Messrs. Lyell and Faraday,* published in the following year, cordially supported the proposal as the most likely means to disseminate a knowledge of the best methods of conducting mining operations, and to put a stop to dangerous practices. At the same time Dr. John Murray came forward in support of the movement, publishing in 1844, in the form of a pamphlet dedicated to Lord Ashley, a series of letters communicated by him to the South Shields Committee. "I freely and frankly confess," he observes in the dedicatory epistle, "that I utterly despair of any amelioration, unless Parliament interfere." Professor Ansted, in like manner, in a paper read at the meeting of the British Association for the Advancement of Science in 1845, expressed his conviction that no great improvements would ever be effected in the working of collieries without some kind of Government interference.

A most powerful argument in favour of those who recommended a comprehensive system of mine supervision authorised by the Legislature was the fact that great explosions were now becoming general in all the coal-fields. Previous to this time nearly all the great explosions had been confined to the collieries of the North of England, which, being the deepest and most extensive in the kingdom, were exposed to the greatest danger from fire-damp. The spread of the railway system, and the rise of steam navigation, however, were followed by a rapid deepening of the mines of the Midland districts and South Wales; and from about the year 1843 great explosions ceased to be peculiar to any particular coal-fields, a considerable proportion of them occurring in localities where they had formerly been almost if not altogether unknown.

The miners too were now looking to the Legislature to assist them amidst the dangers of their occupation; and nothing having resulted from the investigations of Messrs. Lyell and Faraday, another petition was drawn up and presented to the House of Commons in March, 1845. Much interest in the subject was expressed in Parliament, and it having been represented to the Government that the circumstances connected with mine explosions were still imperfectly understood, another commission, consisting of Sir H. T. de la Beche and Dr. Lyon Playfair, was appointed in August of the same year. These gentlemen were directed to inquire into the conditions under which explosive and other gases in mines are generated; to ascertain as far as possible the nature and condition of these gases; and the measures, if any, which can be applied in mitigation, if not in prevention, of the evils inflicted through their agency.

While the commissioners were conducting their inquiry two serious explosions occurred, one at Jarrow Colliery, Durham, and the other at Risca in South Wales, and on both occasions special instructions were issued to the commissioners to hold investigations into the attendant circumstances. The examination in the former case was conducted by Dr. Lyon Playfair and Mr. David Williams, and in the latter by Sir H. T. de la Beche and Mr. Warington Smyth.

The commissioners presented their report on the 1st of June, 1846. After describing the conditions under which noxious gases are evolved in mines, and furnishing analyses of various samples of fire-damp, they proceed to discuss measures for the prevention of accidents. They allude to the alleged insecurity of safety-lamps, but express their opinion, that although they may not be absolutely safe under unusual circumstances, their utility appears sufficiently sanctioned by experience to make them the subject of legislative enactment. They endorse the condemnation of the system of working a colliery by means of a single shaft, the evils of which had recently been witnessed in the case of the explosion at Jarrow; adding that similar dangers exist where two shafts are in use placed close to each other and insufficiently separated, as was the case at Risca. They refer to the great improvements effected in the ventilation of collieries by the employment of ventilating furnaces, more particularly in the North of England, where the further improvement of shortening the air-courses by splitting the air was resorted to; but state, that while examples of good ventilation might be found in some collieries, particularly in certain districts, taken as a whole the general state of the ventilation was very imperfect. With regard to legislative measures, they thought that collieries were worked under such a great variety of conditions that any general system of legislation would be inapplicable; but suggested that this difficulty might be overcome by the subdivision of the kingdom into convenient districts, and the appointment of properly qualified inspectors vested with discretionary powers, so that the needful adjustments to different circumstances might be effected. The necessity of good plans and sections of the collieries they state is sufficiently obvious. In conclusion they recommended that the use of safety-lamps in fiery mines should be made compulsory by the Legislature, and expressed their opinion that the evils existing in the collieries might be at least mitigated by a careful and judicious inspection.

Near the end of the year 1846, explosions having occurred at Rounds Green New Colliery, near Oldbury in Warwickshire, and at the Burgh Colliery, Coppul, near Chorley in Lancashire, Sir H. T. de la Beche and Dr. Playfair were requested by Government to peruse the evidence taken at the inquests, and to advise whether any further inquiry into the circumstances was likely to be attended with beneficial results. Having done so, they recommended that Mr. Warington Smyth should be authorised to examine and report upon the conditions under which these collieries were worked, the system of ventilation pursued, and the lights employed; adding, that further experience served to strengthen their opinion previously expressed, that increased safety in working collieries would be obtained if a careful supervision were established by properly qualified persons. From Mr. Smyth's report, dated 20th January, 1847, it appears that at the former colliery no efficient system of ventilation existed at all; while at the latter, blasting the coal with gunpowder was necessitated by the hardness of the seam, a circumstance which was considered to render the general employment of the Davy lamp impossible.

Another serious explosion having happened at Ardsley Main, or Oaks Colliery, near Barnsley, Yorkshire, in March, 1847, by which seventy-three lives were lost, Sir H. T. de la Beche was instructed to proceed there to investigate the cause of the accident, accompanied by any gentleman he thought fit to associate with himself in the inquiry. He and Mr. Warington Smyth accordingly repaired to Barnsley and examined into the matter, and they drew up a joint report dated 22nd March, 1847. After giving an interesting account of the circumstances connected with the explosion they animadverted upon the shafts being too near to each other (nine feet apart), the force of the blast having made a breach between them at a weak point; expressed their disapproval of naked lights being allowed to be used in proximity to a goaf containing fire-damp—in their opinion the cause of the accident; and reiterated the opinion previously expressed, that "a system of inspection—one not over-meddling, but at the same time securing the most effective ventilation and the proper use of lights —should be adopted."

The appointment of inspectors of mines was warmly advocated by Mr. Seymour Tremenheere, who, during the period of four years in which he had acted as commissioner under Lord Ashley's Act, had had many opportunities of acquainting himself with the unequal character of the management of the mines in different parts of the kingdom. In his report for the year 1847, presented during the month of June, Mr. Tremenheere includes a document containing his views upon this subject which had been supplied to the Home Secretary in February preceding. In this he expresses his conviction that inspection, without compulsory powers of interference, would be unobjectionable and useful, inasmuch as it would diffuse a knowledge of the best plans of ventilation practicable in each district, and lead to many suggestions being made tending to remove known defects, and thereby to diminish the occurrence of fatal accidents; and also would in many cases act as a stimulus even to well-meaning and benevolent employers, by directing their attention to the best means of providing for the health and safety of the people working in their mines.

In the above-mentioned document Mr. Tremenheere furnishes extracts in favour of the appointment of inspectors from a petition about to be presented to Parliament by the Miners' Association, a body numbering some 60,000 members. This petition was laid before Parliament by Mr. Duncombe in May, 1847, and an attempt was made shortly afterwards by the same gentleman to introduce a Bill dealing with the subject, but without success.

The necessity for legislative measures, however, was not lost sight of by the Government, and Mr. Tremenheere was instructed to proceed to France and Belgium to make inquiries into the system of mining inspection in those countries. The results of this visit were communicated to the Home Secretary in a report dated December, 1847. In August of the following year, the same gentleman was instructed to proceed to Germany for a similar purpose, and the information elicited was embodied in a report presented to the Home Secretary, dated November, 1848.

At this stage of matters a heavy explosion occurred at Darley Main Colliery, Barnsley, on the 24th of January, 1849, by which seventy-four persons perished. Mr. Tremenheere and Mr. Warington Smyth were immediately instructed to proceed to the seat of the catastrophe to investigate the circumstances. Among those examined at the inquest were Mr. Nicholas Wood and Mr. B. Biram (who had been summoned by the coroner to examine the works), Mr. Goodwin, Mr. J. T. Woodhouse, and Mr. Warington Smyth. These gentlemen expressed a strong and unanimous opinion that a system of underground inspection on behalf of the Government ought no longer to be delayed—an opinion which was endorsed by the jury in their verdict.

The reports of Mr. Tremenheere and Mr. Smyth were presented in February following; and in consequence of the agitation which continued to be kept up, a few months later two inquiries bearing on the subject were set on foot. On the 15th of June Messrs. J. K. Blackwell and Professor Phillips were appointed by Government to visit the mines in different parts of the kingdom for the purpose of collecting information regarding their condition: their attention being specially directed to the state of the ventilation, and the condition of the mines as to the safety of the workpeople; the chief defects in the modes of carrying on the operations; and what general improvements and precautions might be suggested in their management. Three days later (18th of June), on the motion of Lord Wharncliffe, a Select Committee of the House of Lords was appointed "to inquire into the best means of preventing the occurrence of dangerous accidents in coal mines."

The labours of the Lords' Committee were confined to the examination of witnesses, and extended over four or five weeks. On the 26th of July they drew up a highly judicious report based upon the evidence laid before them. They found that the condition of the mines as respects ventilation differed widely, but was for the most part seriously defective. That the greatest destruction of life, however, did not arise from extensive calamities such as explosions, but from the smaller casualties of continual occurrence, occasioning the loss of a few lives at a time—a fact which had previously been frequently commented upon. They remark upon the striking unanimity of opinion among the witnesses in favour of Government inspection; the majority of the witnesses advocating that inspectors should be invested with no direct powers beyond those of entering and examining mines and inspecting plans, and whose duties should extend to recording and reporting, making suggestions, and communicating information to the managers or owners —a view in which the Committee concurred, and which they thought might gradually accomplish essential improvements in the best manner. They further express their opinion that, taking all the circumstances into account, "it is the imperative duty of Parliament and the executive to adopt, for the purpose of obtaining such security as is undoubtedly within the reach of precaution, any steps, whether of the nature of inspection or of direct enactment, consistent with the free pursuits of industry and commerce, with the mutual relations in this country between the Government and private enterprise, and with the due recognition of that responsibility imposed upon the owners and managers of mines, which it should be the care of all rather to strengthen than to impair." In concluding their report they allude to the want felt in this country of facilities for acquiring instruction such as is provided by the mining schools and colleges established in the principal mining districts of the Continent, apparently with the most beneficial effects.

The task imposed upon Mr. Blackwell and Professor Phillips necessarily occupied some time, and their reports, which were both of a highly able and instructive character, were not laid before Parliament till the 6th of May, 1850. The investigations of these gentlemen served to corroborate the opinions already arrived at by the Select Committee of the House of Lords as to the great inequality which existed in the condition of different mines in regard to safety, and the necessity for a more extended application of the most improved principles, and a better education of the mining population. This, it was pointed out, was all the more essential inasmuch as shallow mines, which were being carried on with comparatively little risk, were certain to become more dangerous as the works were carried to greater depths. Professor Phillips advocated the establishment of mining schools as the means of imparting a due amount of practical and scientific acquirements to the managers of mines; adding, that for securing the right use of this knowledge in the actual management of the mines, a systematic inspection under the authority of Government appeared desirable.

Soon afterwards a measure was brought forward by the Government, which met with comparatively little opposition, and was passed on the 11th of August, under the title of "An Act for the Inspection of Coal Mines in Great Britain." This Act provided for the appointment of inspectors by the Secretary of State, who were to have power to enter and inspect the works of any colliery, both above and below ground, and to inquire into all matters relating to the safety of the workpeople. It also provided for the making and maintaining of correct plans; for notices of accidents causing loss of life being sent within twenty-four hours to one of her Majesty's Secretaries of State, &c.; and was to remain in force for a period of five years. In November following four inspectors were appointed, and two more were added shortly afterwards.

The great frequency with which explosions continued to occur led to the appointment of a Select Committee of the House of Commons on the 27th of May, 1852, who, after holding a very cursory investigation, drew up and presented a report on the 22nd of June. The subject was again referred to a Select Committee in May, 1853, and the inquiry was continued by another Committee appointed in February, 1854, who presented their final report in June following. While differing in opinion on some technical questions, the Committees were agreed upon the main points at issue, and alike advocated the necessity for improved ventilation, efficient supervision, increased inspection, and better education. In accordance with the further information which had been obtained, the Act of Parliament was modified on its renewal in 1855, seven general rules being added, and provision made for the establishment of codes of special rules applicable to each colliery. The number of inspectors was also increased to twelve. In 1860 the Act was further amended and made perpetual, and the office of inspector under Lord Ashley's Act was abolished.

Notwithstanding the oft-repeated condemnation of the system of working collieries by means of a single bratticed shaft, no steps had yet been taken to put an end to the practice. In January, 1862, however, the long list of calamities arising from this defective arrangement culminated in the great catastrophe at Hartley Colliery, in Northumberland, when two hundred and four persons lost their lives by the half of the beam of the pumping-engine breaking off and falling down the pit, wrecking the brattice, and destroying the ventilation, and cutting off all communication with the surface. This at length led to the passing of a short Act of Parliament prohibiting collieries from being worked unless provided with at least two means of exit, separated by not less than ten feet of natural strata.

The operation of the Act of 1860 "for the Regulation and Inspection of Mines," was made the subject of inquiry by a Select Committee of the House of Commons appointed for the purpose in 1865, who in their report presented in July, 1867, suggested a number of alterations in the then existing law; but no change was effected till 1872. On the 10th of August in this year the present "Coal Mines Regulation Act" received the royal assent, and came into operation in England and Scotland on the 1st of January, 1873, and in Ireland on the 1st of January, 1874. No increase was made in the number of chief inspectors, but each of the previously existing inspectors was provided with an assistant.

The appointment of inspectors of mines by Government, in 1850, was followed by the opening of the Royal

School of Mines, London, in 1851, and by the establishment of the first Mining Institute at Newcastle-on Tyne, in 1852, under the presidency of Mr. Nicholas Wood, originally with the title of "The North of England Institute of Mining Engineers, and others interested in the prevention of Accidents in Mines, and in the advancement of Mining Science generally." Since this period similar institutes have been established in most of the mining districts, and mining schools, or classes, have been opened at a number of the most important centres—Bristol, Wigan, Newcastle-on-Tyne, &c. A School of Mines was organised at Glasgow in 1859, and carried on for a few years by aid of voluntary subscriptions, but it was found necessary to abandon the scheme, as the institution failed to become self-supporting.

CHAPTER XXI.

GREAT IMPROVEMENT IN THE VENTILATION OF COLLIERIES.—THE STEAM JET TRIED AND ABANDONED.—MECHANICAL VENTILATORS COME INTO EXTENSIVE USE.

"There is a spirit of intelligent energy now awakened with reference to this object, from which the best results may hereafter be expected."—*Report of the Lords' Committee*, 1849.

DURING the course of the present century the ideas entertained regarding the ventilation of mines have undergone a wonderful revolution, and the extraordinary volumes of air which now sweep through the best-conducted collieries present a striking contrast to the meagre air-currents of the commencement of the century. The life of Mr. Buddle may be regarded as forming the connecting link between the old *régime* and the new one; the system of compound ventilation, or "splitting the air," introduced by him, was the first step in the direction of improvement, and inaugurated a new era in mine ventilation.

Accustomed, however, as Mr. Buddle was in his youth to the insignificant volumes of air which could alone be introduced into the mines under the system of coursing the air in a single current through the whole length of the workings, and having introduced the new system of ventilation rather with a view to overcoming difficulties connected with the use of the ventilating furnace than with the object of obtaining an increased volume of air, it is perhaps not surprising that he continued throughout most of his life to entertain what to us appear inadequate views on the subject. In 1813, in his communication to Sir Ralph Milbanke, president of the Sunderland Society, he observes that the standard air-current employed in the ventilation of the collieries under his care abounding in inflammable gas moved through an aperture from thirty to forty feet in area, with a velocity of three feet per second, the volume of air being from 5,400 to 7,200 cubic feet per minute. In this standard air-current Mr. Buddle conceived that a maximum of efficiency had been reached, and that in this direction no further improvement could be looked for. Even in 1835 the total volume of air employed to ventilate Wallsend Colliery, with three downcast and two upcast pits, only amounted to 5,000 cubic feet per minute. There is little reason to doubt that inadequate ventilation had much to do with the great loss of life which occurred in the collieries under Mr. Buddle's superintendence. His career was a long and distinguished one, but notwithstanding his great skill and care, and his indefatigable attention to his duties, no fewer than 840 persons are stated to have perished in the pits of which he was viewer.

It was in the newer collieries of the Wear district—where splitting the air was introduced about 1820—that a commencement was first made to employ volumes of air vastly greater than had been thought of before. This was effected by enlarging the shafts and air-ways, increasing the number of splits and shortening their run, and constructing more capacious (and sometimes several) furnaces. In many cases also great assistance was obtained from the fires of boilers placed underground in connection with steam machinery for hauling the coal, which was coming into common use as a substitute for horses. In 1835, while Mr. Buddle, as we have seen, was ventilating Wallsend Colliery with 5,000 cubic feet of air per minute, at Pensher Colliery (where a special shaft had been sunk for ventilating purposes) the aggregate volume of air sweeping through the mine amounted to 51,900 cubic feet per minute; and at Hetton Colliery at the same time the ventilating current had reached 96,300 cubic feet per minute.

The movement in the direction of better ventilation having once been initiated, the viewers of the period vied with each other in introducing larger and larger volumes of air into the mines, and the above figures were soon left behind. In a statement of the quantities of air circulating through some of the most important collieries in the North of England in 1850, we find Hetton with 190,000 cubic feet, South Hetton and Murton with 132,895 cubic feet, and Wallsend with 121,360 cubic feet per minute.

Within ten or twelve years later the ventilating currents at Hetton Colliery underwent a further enormous augmentation. The ventilating power employed consisted of four furnaces and three boiler fires at Hetton, two furnaces and two boiler fires at Elemore, and one furnace and six boiler fires at Eppleton; and the quantity of air passing through the pits reached the vast total of 450,000 cubic feet per minute.

Among notable instances of furnace ventilation at the present time we have South Hetton and Murton Collieries, with three furnaces and twelve boiler fires, emitting from 380,000 to 440,000 cubic feet; the deep pit at Rosebridge, Wigan, giving, with two furnaces, 235,000 cubic feet; and Wynnstay Colliery, North Wales, with a single furnace, 200,000 cubic feet per minute.

Though furnaces still present the most powerful means of obtaining large volumes of air in the case of deep and dry upcast pits, their use is not free from a number of serious drawbacks. Unless fed with fresh air direct from the downcast pit there is a certain amount of risk of their giving rise to explosion; and if they be not securely isolated from the surrounding strata there is danger of their setting fire to coal seams in their vicinity. Considerable difficulty also exists in executing repairs in the furnace drifts and upcast shafts; while the volumes of smoke poured into the shaft render a furnace upcast a very objectionable passage for the men to traverse in entering or leaving the mine. In addition to this, the operation of relighting the furnace and restoring the ventilation after an accident has occurred is a task of much anxiety and no small danger. These and similar considerations have served as a powerful stimulus to the application of other methods of effecting the ventilation of coal mines.

The experiments made by Mr. Buddle at the commencement of the century were considered to have established the superiority of the furnace over the substitutes which he attempted to employ in lieu of it, but the desirability of excluding fire as much as possible from collieries yielding inflammable gas, continued to lead to various proposals with this object being brought forward from time to time. Mr. Goldsworthy Gurney's scheme for employing jets of high-pressure steam, and Mr. John Martin's proposal to employ a large exhausting fan, both laid before the Select Committee of the House of Commons in 1835, have been already adverted to. These suggestions met with little approval at the time from the mining community, but no long period elapsed before the idea of employing substitutes for the furnace began to be more favourably entertained. The steam jet was strongly recommended by the South Shields Committee in their report published in 1843, and a few years afterwards it came to be actually applied to the ventilation of mines, the first trial of it being made by Mr. T. E. Forster, at Seaton Delaval Colliery, Northumberland, in 1848.

Mr. Forster was led to adopt the steam-jet system of ventilation from having witnessed some experiments at the Polytechnic establishment in London, in June, 1848, with which he was favourably impressed. In November following he applied it in an upcast pit where two boilers already existed having a greater steam-producing capacity than was required for the work they had to perform.

At first the new system promised to be a success, and the favourable accounts of it given by Mr. Forster led to its being adopted at a number of other collieries, viz., Belmont, North Hetton, Usworth, Norwood, &c. But at Seaton Delaval the jet apparatus was applied under peculiar circumstances, there being four downcast pits supplying air to one upcast, and it was not found to give such good results at other places.

The question of the comparative merits of the steam jet and the furnace excited much interest among mining engineers, perhaps more particularly on account of the emphatic approval of the former by the Select

Committee of the House of Commons in 1852. The subject was widely discussed and experimented upon, and formed the topic of the first papers read before the North of England Institute in 1852-3. But the numerous elaborate and exhaustive experiments which were made at this time, particularly by Mr. Nicholas Wood, served to establish the undoubted superiority of the furnace both as regards efficiency and economy, and the short-lived popularity of the steam jet speedily came to an end.

While steam-jet ventilation was undergoing its trial in the north, a more important innovation on furnace ventilation was being introduced in South Wales. This consisted in the employment of mechanical ventilators driven by steam-engines. These had been in use for a considerable time on the Continent, particularly at the collieries in Belgium, but their regular employment in this country only commenced in 1849, in the early part of which year one of Struvé's air-pump machines, and one of Brunton's revolving fans, were erected simultaneously at collieries in Glamorganshire. The former, as first applied at Eaglesbush Colliery, near Neath, consisted of two double-acting airometers, each twelve feet in diameter, and having a stroke of from four to six feet. The latter consisted of a horizontal fan twenty-two feet in diameter, running on a vertical spindle, and placed over the top of the upcast shaft; the first machine being erected at Mr. Powell's Gellygaer Colliery.

During the next few years the use of mechanical ventilators gradually extended. A number of Struvé's and Brunton's machines, of various sizes, were built at different collieries in Wales; and in 1852 a form of straight-vaned fan resembling Brunton's, but having the axis horizontal, was introduced by Mr. James Nasmyth; the first being applied at one of Earl Fitzwilliam's collieries, near Rotherham. This fan was only six feet in diameter, but larger sizes were built by Nasmyth shortly afterwards; one being erected at Abercarn, in Glamorganshire, about 1853-4, with a diameter of $13\frac{1}{2}$ feet and a width of 3 feet, followed by a still larger one built for Earl Fitzwilliam. A fan having tangential blades was invented and patented in 1853 by Mr. Biram (viewer to Earl Fitzwilliam), who in the course of the next three or four years applied various fans to ventilate collieries at Elsecar.

The utility of mechanical ventilators was brought before the North of England Institute of Mining Engineers in 1858 by Mr. J. J. Atkinson, Inspector of Mines—a gentleman whose valuable papers contributed from time to time to the *Transactions* of this Institute served to throw much light on the subject of mine ventilation—in a paper entitled "On the comparative consumption of fuel by ventilating furnaces and ventilating machines, when used to ventilate mines." In this paper Mr. Atkinson adduced statistics exhibiting the superiority of machines in point of economy. As yet no mechanical ventilators had been applied in the Great Northern coal-field, but their introduction took place soon afterwards, an open running fan, similar to those at Elsecar, being erected at Tursdale Colliery, Durham, about 1860.

From this time large numbers of mechanical ventilators of various types came into use. The Guibal fan, with spiral case and flexible shutter (the invention of M. Guibal, of Mons), was patented in 1862, and introduced at Elswick Colliery, near Newcastle-on-Tyne, about 1864, and came so rapidly into favour that within ten or twelve years no fewer than two hundred were at work at collieries in different parts of the kingdom. The Schiele fan, brought forward immediately after the Guibal, and of the same type, has also come into extended use. Waddle fans, open at the periphery and without any exterior casing, have likewise been erected at many collieries. Among other machines of different forms which have been applied to a smaller extent, may be mentioned Lemielle's feathering fan, Nixon's horizontal air-pump piston machine the revolving drum machines of Cooke, and Root's machine resembling in principle the pneumatic wheels of M. Fabry used at collieries on the Continent.

The fear formerly entertained of interruptions to the ventilation being occasioned by mechanical ventilators breaking down, was gradually dispelled as their application was extended, and they were proved by experience to be capable of performing their work with regularity, economy, efficiency, and safety. Of late they have come to be regarded with more and more favour, and are being so largely introduced as almost to promise ultimately to supersede furnaces altogether. The rapidity with which they have recently been adopted is forcibly exhibited by the evidence of some of the witnesses examined by the Royal Commissioners now inquiring into the subject of accidents in mines. Thus Mr. Ralph Moore, inspector of mines for the eastern division of Scotland, stated that the number of fans in use in his district had increased from one in 1873 to upwards of ninety in 1879. Similar testimony in regard to the fan gradually superseding the furnace was afforded by various witnesses, who expressed a remarkable unanimity of opinion in favour of the change.

Of the three forms of fan most commonly used in this country, viz., the Guibal, the Waddle, and the Schiele, the latter is rarely made of a greater diameter than sixteen feet, and is made to revolve with great velocity; while the Waddle and the Guibal are constructed of all sizes up to fifty feet diameter; the latter being frequently from twelve to fifteen feet in breadth, and capable of producing a ventilating current of upwards of 200,000 cubic feet per minute.

CHAPTER XXII.

RECENT INVENTIONS, EXPERIMENTS, AND IMPROVEMENTS.

NOTABLE among the improvements effected of recent years, in the winning and working of collieries, may be mentioned the system of sinking through heavily watered strata invented by Messrs. Kind and Chaudron, which, after being successfully applied in many difficult cases on the Continent, has lately been introduced into this country. The system consists in boring out the shaft from the surface, until the watery strata have been pierced, and a suitable foundation obtained on which to place the cast-iron tubbing. The tubbing, composed of rings the full size of the shaft, is then lowered into position, and by means of an ingenious stuffing-box arrangement at the bottom, packed with moss, a water-tight joint is formed as soon as it rests upon the bed prepared for it. The water contained in the shaft is then removed, and sinking in the dry measures carried on after the ordinary fashion.

By the aid of the above system, sinkings have been effected at Cannock Chase, in Staffordshire, and at Whitburn, in Durham, under circumstances in which the usual methods were found inadequate to contend with the great quantities of water encountered. Instead of being a hindrance, the water in the shaft assists in the process of boring, and its quantity is immaterial, inasmuch as it is never removed from the shaft until the exterior feeders have been effectually dammed back. The difficulties at Whitburn were even more formidable than those encountered at Murton. The influx of water into the shafts amounted to nearly 12,000 gallons per minute, and the attempt to sink by ordinary methods was abandoned as impracticable. The Kind-Chaudron system was then brought into play, and with such success, that when the first pit was completed through the watery strata, the water which found its way into it only amounted to a little over one gallon per minute.

In the fittings of shafts a variety of innovations have been made within the last twenty or thirty years. The wood guides at first employed have in many instances, more especially in particular districts, been superseded by tightly-stretched iron-wire ropes, or by rolled iron rails of various sections; while since the increased abundance and lessened cost of steel, consequent upon the invention of the Bessemer process, this material, on account of its superior strength and lightness, has come to be employed to a considerable extent, in lieu of iron, in the construction of winding ropes and cages, as well as for numerous other purposes.

The general introduction of guides and cages was followed by the invention of many forms of "safety cages," designed to suspend themselves upon the guides in the event of the rope breaking. Among the earliest was that of Mr. Fourdrinier, of Staffordshire, patented in 1847. Between the years 1854–64, in particular, much attention was given to the subject, and safety-cages, on different principles of action, were applied in practice to a considerable extent, *e.g.* White and Grant's, Owen's, Aytoun's, Knowles', Calow's, &c. It is admitted that several accidents were prevented by their use; but, on the other hand, mischief was occasionally caused by the suspending apparatus coming into play when not wanted, and it was sometimes found to be out of order when wanted; so that their success was at best equivocal, and their popularity gradually waned. They are now little, if at all, used in the collieries of this country, it being considered preferable, where winding is carried on with rapidity, to place reliance upon ropes of the best material, carefully tended, and not over-long run.

The use of "safety-hooks" for the prevention of over-winding is regarded with more favour. These are designed to disconnect the cage from the rope, and suspend it at the same time, on its being drawn within dangerous proximity to the pulleys. Various forms, invented by Messrs. Bryham, Ormerod, Walker, &c., are now extensively employed at many of the deepest and most important collieries.

A method of counterbalancing the weight of the winding ropes, by suspending a "tail rope" below the cages (which was made the subject of a patent, by Burrows, in 1856), has of late years been making its way into use, and is found to be simple, inexpensive, and effective.

A new form of winding apparatus, the invention of Herr Koepe, engineer to Messrs. Krupp and Co., in which the counterbalance rope forms an essential feature, has been employed for some years on the Continent, and more recently in this country. It consists in substituting for the drum usually employed, a large pulley, having a wooden rim with a deep groove in it. The winding rope merely passes round the pulley, thus forming with the counterbalance an endless-rope arrangement, broken only by the cages, which constitute links between the upper and lower loops, the apparatus being at all points in perfect equilibrium.

It is obvious that without additional precautionary measures, both cages would fall to the bottom in the event of a breakage of the rope taking place, but this danger is overcome by the employment of safety-ropes, which, under ordinary circumstances, run freely in the shaft, but serve to suspend the cages on an accident occurring to the main winding rope. The Koepe system has been in use for some time at Bestwood Colliery, Nottingham, where it is stated to have given every satisfaction.

In the haulage of the coal carriages along the main underground roads, horses have to a great extent been superseded by machinery, usually consisting of wire ropes, of iron or steel, or chains, worked by steam-engines placed either at the surface or in the mine. In the case of level or undulating roads, tail ropes, endless ropes, and endless chains, are variously employed, to effect the haulage of the carriages, in both directions, to and from the workings.

In some instances compressed air, supplied from machinery at the surface, has been applied to the working of hauling engines placed at different points in the mine. This agent was first applied at Govan Colliery, near Glasgow, in 1849, to actuate an underground winding engine, the machinery being supplied by Messrs. Randolph, Elder, and Co. More recently, air-compressing machinery has been erected at a number of collieries for haulage and other purposes. But though the system was attended with considerable success, and was applicable in situations where the use of steam was inadmissible, it involved a greater outlay of capital, and an increased tear and wear of machinery, which added to the loss of power in compressing the air, makes it unable to compete with other methods in point of economy under ordinary circumstances.

Some attempts have been made to apply small locomotive engines to the work of underground haulage. In Messrs. Lishman and Young's arrangement, which has been in use at Bunker Hill Colliery, Durham, for some years, compressed air stored in a tank is the motive power employed; but this class of machine can scarcely be considered to have as yet passed beyond the experimental stage.

The invention of a machine for performing the most laborious and monotonous part of the work of the collier—that of holing or undercutting the coal—has exercised the ingenuity of inventive minds for a very long period, and more particularly within the last twenty years, since Messrs. Donisthorpe, Firth, and Ridley's machine demonstrated the practicability of the scheme. This machine, patented in 1861, and consisting of picks driven by compressed air, was applied at West Ardsley Colliery, near Leeds, and successfully performed the work of undercutting the coal. It was subsequently improved by its inventors, and remained in use at West Ardsley many years, and was only discontinued, we believe, on account of difficulties with the workmen. A similar machine (Firth's) is still at work at Hetton Colliery, Durham, where it has been at work since 1863.

Other coal-cutting machines, in great variety, have since been brought forward, consisting for the most part of slotting or planing machines, and rotary saws, or cutters, actuated by compressed air. Among those of the latter description, Messrs. Winstanley and Barker's machine, the Gartsherrie (or Baird's) machine, and one or two others have been applied to a considerable extent in practice, and with a fair measure of success. But the superiority of the machines to the ordinary method of getting the coal by manual labour has not been so decided as to lead to their extended use.

During the long interval that has transpired since the invention of the Davy lamp, innumerable varieties of safety-lamps have been produced, founded upon the principle of security discovered by Sir Humphry Davy. Of these, the Clanny, Stephenson, and Mueseler lamps (the latter the only form of safety-lamp allowed to be employed in the mines of Belgium), are the most extensively used in this country next to the "Davy." In the Clanny and Mueseler lamps a cylinder of thick glass takes the place of the lower part of the cylinder of wire gauze, which enables them to afford a superior light; while these lamps, in common with the "Stephenson," become readily extinguished in the presence of fire-damp—a circumstance which causes them to be preferred in collieries subject to sudden "outbursts" of inflammable gas. In point of simplicity, however—a matter of no small consequence in an instrument of the kind—the original "Davy," in the form in which it left the hands of its inventor, has never yet been excelled, and still affords the best means of discovering the presence of fire-damp. To guard the lamp more effectually against currents of explosive mixture, the plan of enclosing it completely in a case, partially constructed of glass (being in fact only a further extension of the shield principle suggested by Sir Humphry Davy), has been lately introduced. This form of lamp, known as the "tin can safety-lamp," is now extensively used in the Durham collieries, and according to the recently-published preliminary report of the Royal Commissioners, this simple expedient transforms the Davy lamp, "from an instrument of the utmost danger, in a rapid current, into one of great security."

In one or two instances, as at Pleasley Colliery, Nottingham, Risca Colliery, in South Wales, and Earnock Colliery, Lanarkshire, the electric light has been introduced underground, but only by way of experiment, and chiefly in the lighting of main roads. Whether insulated electric lamps will eventually supersede the safety-lamps at present in use is a problem which awaits solution in the future.

For purposes of signalling on engine planes, and in some cases also in the shaft, electricity has already been in use for a number of years.

CHAPTER XXIII.

MODERN MINING.—MEASURES OF SAFETY AGAINST EXPLOSION.

THE deep sinkings approaching to 300 fathoms made in the Great Northern coal-field, at Monkwearmouth, Seaham, Ryhope, &c., about the middle of the present century, have been followed by a still deeper range of sinkings, in which the pits of the Lancashire and Cheshire coal-field have taken the lead. Here the Astley deep pit at Dukinfield reached a depth of 350 fathoms in 1858; at Rosebridge, Wigan, a depth of 408 fathoms was attained in 1869; and more recently the new winning at the Ashton Moss Colliery, Audenshaw, near Manchester, has been carried down considerably further, the "Great Mine" coal having been sunk to on the 5th of March, 1881, at the depth of 448 fathoms.

Coincidently with the deepening of the mines, a continual enlargement of the shafts has been going on; and while at the commencement of the century a diameter of 12 feet was considered a suitable size for pits of 100 fathoms depth, at the present day the Lancashire pits are being made 16 or 18 feet in diameter, to work the coal lying at depths of from 200 to 400 fathoms, and in a few instances even larger sizes have been adopted.

The improvements in the mechanical engineering of collieries have more than kept pace with the increasing depth of the mines, and by means of powerful winding engines (reaching at times as much as 1,500 horse-power), acting directly on drums from 15 to 30 feet in diameter, coals are drawn at many important collieries at the rate of 100 tons or more per hour: the cage, with its load of four, six, or eight carriages, containing two or three tons of coal, travelling in the quickest part of its run at the speed of a mile per minute, or equal to that of an express train. Thus outputs of from 1,200 to 1,800 tons of coal per day are in many cases obtained from a single shaft.

Hence, though the depth of the mines is continually increasing, the quantity of coal drawn is likewise increasing from year to year, until the recently published returns for 1881 show the vast production of 154,184,300 tons per annum; the collieries giving employment to nearly half a million of persons.

Though an important move in the direction of greater safety in working coal mines was made when the single bratticed pit was abolished, and two separate shafts substituted for it, much of the security obtainable from this arrangement is lost when the two shafts, as is usually the case, are sunk in close proximity to each other. It has been forcibly urged, from time to time, by the most eminent authorities, that the greater the distance between the downcast and the upcast, the more chance of escape is afforded to the pitmen in case of accident. On the other hand, it is contended that to place the shafts a long distance apart would involve a still further delay in the already long period required to open out deep collieries. This difficulty might of course be overcome by the employment of a third shaft, but a still better arrangement, now sometimes adopted, in the case of extensive royalties, is to connect together a pair of downcast and a pair of upcast shafts, the latter each provided with a ventilator so placed as to be applicable to exhaust either from one or both pits. When these pairs of pits are made of ample size, and situated as far apart as possible, this arrangement seems to leave little to be desired in point of efficiency and safety, so far as shafts are concerned.

That large volumes of air suitably distributed through the workings of a mine constitutes the main factor in reducing to a minimum the risk of explosion, is a matter which will probably be generally admitted. But the importance of employing capacious shafts to effect this is perhaps underrated. Hence it sometimes occurs that a considerable proportion of the ventilating power is expended in forcing the air-current at a high velocity through shafts of inadequate area, thus reducing to a large extent the quantity of air which, under better auspices, might be made available for the ventilation of the workings.

The desirability if not absolute necessity of excluding blasting with gunpowder from fiery mines, has from time to time been strenuously insisted upon. When the safety-lamp was first introduced, its use was considered to be incompatible with the employment of gunpowder in coal getting. On this plea, for example, Mr. Buddle continued to work Jarrow Colliery with naked lights, and in 1834 a sudden discharge of inflammable gas occurred, and an explosion inevitably ensued. At the present day, in many instances, blasting is continued (under certain restrictions) in mines where safety-lamps are exclusively employed. Whether under any restrictions such an arrangement is consistent with reason is a point regarding which much diversity of opinion exists. To record minute variations in the rise and fall of the barometer and thermometer, to examine and securely lock safety-lamps with the utmost attention and care, and at the same time to admit into the recesses of the workings the great open flame of gunpowder, seems to savour of what is usually described as straining at a gnat and swallowing a camel. That blasting has to answer for a long catalogue of explosions is a fact which will scarcely be disputed.

Much attention has been directed of late to the probability of coal-dust playing an important part in propagating indefinitely the flame arising from a small local explosion, whether of gunpowder or fire-damp. Herein it is supposed lies the secret of the mysterious violence which has characterized some explosions, which have occurred under circumstances where it appeared almost impossible to account for the presence of a volume of fire-damp sufficient to produce the results. Explosions in which dust is supposed to be almost, if not altogether, independent of fire-damp, are considered to have their origin in the blast of a charge of gunpowder, which raises the dust and ignites it at the same time; more especially when the full force of the gunpowder is expended in blowing out the stemming or tamping, and producing what is termed a " blown-out shot." The same results, it is stated, may also be produced by the occurrence of a small local explosion of fire-damp in a dry and dusty mine. Should this be so, another powerful argument against the continuance of blasting in fiery mines will have been added to the list of those already existing; while, at the same time, there appears to be a necessity for the adoption of measures of precaution, whether by watering the roads or otherwise, to check the raising of the dust, in order that local explosions may be prevented from developing into general ones.

Various substitutes for gunpowder have been

suggested, such as compressed air cartridges, water cartridges, &c., and more recently the use of caustic lime. A process resembling the latter method was employed by miners in breaking up rock previous to the introduction of blasting powder. Should any system of effecting this, without the production of flame, be found suitable for application in practice, another highly important step towards increased safety against explosions will have been achieved.

The liability of coal mines to be suddenly inundated by great volumes of gas instantaneously liberated, either from the seam in course of working, or from a contiguous fiery seam, was long regarded with incredulity even by many well-informed persons. The actual existence of such a danger, however, is now too well established to admit of a doubt, and in some cases precautionary measures are adopted to guard against it. When these " outbursts " of gas proceed from the seam being worked, they appear for the most part to be connected with small fissures running in a direction nearly parallel to the cleavage of the coal. Such outbursts have occurred at a number of collieries on the Tyne, as Jarrow, Walker, and Hebburn, and have in some instances forced a passage through a considerable thickness of coal. To guard against casualties from this cause, borings are sometimes kept in advance of leading excavations driven across the cleavage of the coal, a precaution which can be rendered still more effectual by insulating such exploring drifts from the main body of the workings, and supplying them with a ventilating current of their own.

In like manner when discharges of gas from the floor are to be feared, proceeding from fiery seams lying underneath, borings downwards at intervals are now made in some of the collieries in the midland districts, and large quantities of gas are sometimes liberated by this means; and in addition to such precautions, ventilation by mechanical means, the employment of safety lamps of the self-extinguishing type, or of adequately protected Davy lamps, the abolition of shot-firing, or its restriction to the utmost possible extent, are being recognised as essential to safety, in the case of mines so situated.

After all has been done that can be done to reduce the risk of explosion, by ample and unceasing ventilation, good arrangements, careful and unremitting vigilance, the use of safety-lamps that will not pass explosion in a rapid current, even supplemented by the abolition of shot-firing and the elimination of ventilating furnaces, certain contingencies remain which may at any time lead to disaster, unless, indeed, accumulations of gas can be effectually prevented from taking place. But apart from the possibility of the air-current being rendered temporarily explosive by a sudden outburst of gas, this may be brought about in a variety of other ways, as by derangement of the ventilating machinery, falls of stone obstructing the air-way, or damaging stoppings, or forcing out gas from the goaves, &c.; while a safety-lamp wilfully tampered with or accidentally damaged, or even a spark from a miner's pick, may supply the materials of ignition before the danger has been discovered.[1] It therefore is of the utmost consequence in laying out the workings of a fiery mine, to adopt such arrangements as will confine the fatal effects of explosion within the narrowest possible limits. This consideration has been urged with sufficient frequency by those best conversant with the subject, but want of attention to these warnings has, it is to be feared, too often resulted in great sacrifice of life, which might have been in part at least prevented.

That the large proportion of lives lost is not due to the immediate ignition of the gas, or to the blast of the explosion, but to its secondary consequences, in destroying doors, stoppings, and crossings, has been pointed out again and again. It is not the flame, but the after-damp, and suspension of ventilation, that usually bring about the great havoc of life attendant upon explosion, the proportion of deaths due to the latter being at times as high as seven-eighths of the whole. Hence the necessity of dividing the workings into separate and distinct panels, or districts, protected by barriers of solid coal, to

---

[1] Several instances are recorded of explosions having been caused by a flash of lightning.

prevent, as much as possible, the effects of an explosion from spreading into contiguous parts of a mine, and of so fortifying all stoppings and crossings as to make them able to withstand the force of a blast, in order that derangements of the ventilation may be rectified with the least possible delay.

Considering all the circumstances, it is perhaps too much to expect that the time will come when explosions in coal mines will entirely cease to occur; but the spread of education and intelligence, and the growth of facilities for obtaining a knowledge of the means best calculated to promote the safety of the miners, are sufficient to encourage the hope that, in the future, mining operations may be attended with less risk and loss of life than has hitherto been the case. With the earnest wish that this may hereafter be attained, the writer would bring to a close his endeavour to elucidate the history of coal mining in this country.

THE END.

www.ingramcontent.com/pod-product-compliance
Lightning Source LLC
Chambersburg PA
CBHW031929230426
43672CB00010B/1863